# A New Start

## Refresher A2

### Teaching Guide

D1731307

Cornelsen

**A New Start Refresher A2**
**Teaching Guide**

**Verfasser:**............................. Jürgen Ettenauer, Erding
Claire Holfelder, Speyer

**Redaktion:**............................. Mindy Ehrhart Krull

**Verlagsredaktion:**...................... Meike Kolle, Rebecca Syme

**Illustrationen:**......................... Linden Artists, London (Photocopiables 5 und 11)
Henning Ziegler, Berlin (Photocopiable 2)

**Projektleitung:**........................ Scott Tokaryk

**Umschlaggestaltung:**.................. Klein & Halm Grafikdesign, Berlin

**Layout und technische Umsetzung:**.... zweiband.media, Berlin

**www.cornelsen.de**

Die Links zu externen Webseiten Dritter, die in diesem Lehrwerk angegeben sind,
wurden vor Drucklegung sorgfältig auf ihre Aktualität geprüft. Der Verlag übernimmt
keine Gewähr für die Aktualität und den Inhalt dieser Seiten oder solcher, die mit ihnen
verlinkt sind.

1. Auflage, 1. Druck 2013

Alle Drucke dieser Auflage sind inhaltlich unverändert
und können im Unterricht nebeneinander verwendet werden.

© 2013 Cornelsen Schulverlage GmbH, Berlin

Druck: Himmer AG, Augsburg

ISBN 978-3-464-20037-7

 Inhalt gedruckt auf säurefreiem Papier aus nachhaltiger Forstwirtschaft.

# OVERVIEW

**O**

## Why a new edition of A New Start?

The highly successful *A New Start* programme has, over many years, met the needs of learners of English who wish to build on their existing foreign language competence. However, all living languages evolve. Themes that were once highly topical are replaced by new ones. Recent methodological approaches and studies in language learning and teaching bring about changes within the classroom.

The fundamental methodology of the previous *A New Start Refresher A2* has been maintained in creating this new edition of *A New Start Refresher A2: Coursebook with Grammar and Vocabulary Booklet*. This has provided not only the opportunity to thoroughly revise, refresh and update both the content and design of the original book, but also to give an even clearer, more modern approach to the whole course, bearing in mind the requirements of the *Common European Framework of Reference for Languages*.

*A New Start Refresher A2* offers key scenarios, structures and vocabulary in ten carefully structured units, each consisting of two parts which share the unit's topic. Subjects cover stimulating cultural as well as social issues and situations, providing the learners with useful language and insights into the global English-speaking world. Special emphasis is placed on the significance of English as a lingua franca. To maintain students' motivation levels, there are plenty of task-based activities promoting authentic and meaningful classroom communication.

## Level A2 in the *Common European Framework of Reference for Languages (CEFR)*

*A New Start Refresher A2* adheres to the Level A2 requirements of the *Common European Framework of Reference for Languages* and is aimed at adults who would like to brush up on their skills and boost their language competence to a basic proficiency level.

Level A2 in the *CEFR* means that the students can understand sentences and frequently used expressions related to areas most relevant to them. They can also fulfil tasks requiring a simple and direct exchange of information on familiar and routine subjects. Furthermore, they can describe in simple terms aspects of their background, daily environment and matters of immediate need.

More information about the *CEFR* is available from the Council of Europe at: www.coe.int/t/dg4/linguistic/Cadre1_en.asp

## The structure of a coursebook unit

Every aspect of the previous edition has been reviewed with respect to its topics as well as its methodology. Tried and tested approaches have been retained and continue to form a mainstay of the unit structures, but you can also find major changes and small alterations which have been carried out in order to bring texts and topics, activities and tasks, as well as photos and illustrations, up to date.

Each unit part is designed so that it can be completed in about 90 minutes, i.e. one double lesson. In all, the coursebook offers material for approximately 24 to 26 double lessons but can be extended with the additional online material, e.g. business options.

Each unit is broken down into the following activity types:

**Focus**  The Focus sections introduce the theme, providing the situational presentation of structures and phrases in informative and natural-sounding texts.

**Language Box**  The Language Boxes highlight the structures and phrases focussed on and provide concise explanations. The tick boxes and gaps below the actual examples and explanations are intended to increase the students' awareness of the grammar points and their rules. At the bottom of each Language Box there is a cross reference to the *Grammar and Vocabulary Booklet* containing further grammar explanations and practice possibilities. These are designed as self-study activities for which a full key is provided for students to correct themselves. Encourage students to do these activities on their own and invite them to ask you for clarification in a subsequent class if they don't understand the solutions provided.

**Practice**  The Practice sections provide guided activities for balanced practice of the presented structures.

**Tune In**  These classic listening activities provide the students with the opportunity to hear natural conversations and hone their listening skills.

**Let's Talk**  The Let's Talk activities focus on practising speaking skills and engage students in stimulating learner-centred tasks. In doing so, they recycle language material, provide integrated skills training and draw on scenarios or scripts of interactive exchanges.

**Sound Check**  The Sound Check activities focus on practising and improving intonation, while raising students' awareness of possible phonetic errors which may hinder communication.

**Out and about**  Up-to-date and relevant topics are provided on English-speaking countries and their cultures. These activities are designed to provide a unique angle on the cultural themes and are backed up by supplementary activities and tasks.

**English near me**  This new feature presents interviews with interesting people who bring the cultures of English-speaking countries to the German-speaking world.

**Culture Tips**  These tips provide students with useful insights into distinctive cultural features and social conventions. They aim to raise students' awareness of appropriate intercultural behaviour in English-speaking surroundings.

**Home study**  Each unit part has its own Home study page. In Part A students can find guided vocabulary and grammar activities. Part B provides a longer reading text with a variety of pre- and post-reading tasks. Recordings of these texts are on the CD included in the coursebook so that students can listen to them and thus have the opportunity to hear different accents and dialects. The coursebook also includes a full key to all the activities on the Home study pages.

**Lerntipp**  A *Lerntipp* in German appears in the Home study page in Part A of each unit. These tips suggest additional ways of learning English and aim to motivate students to expose themselves to English without becoming daunted by, for example, fast-speaking news presenters or difficult articles in authentic newspapers.

Additional material can also be found online:

**The website** www.cornelsen.de/newstart
The revised webpage dedicated to *A New Start* contains online exercises and placement tests for students, worksheets, business option worksheets, the complete audio files as MP3s and an extended version of each *English near me* interview.

## What is in the Teaching Guide?

The aim of the *Teaching Guide* is to help you effectively and efficiently prepare for classes and maximize the material provided in the coursebook. Each unit part appears on a double spread, and is thus specifically designed to be a convenient reference for you while preparing and/or teaching. The double spread includes full teaching notes on each activity as well as answer keys that are always located in the bottom right-hand corner for quick reference when reviewing answers with your class. In addition, the Teaching Guide offers useful extra information on cultural and linguistic issues as well as further practical suggestions and tips, including the new features listed below.

**Class opener**  A short introductory activity to each unit part that is either related to the previous unit part or a homework suggestion, or which is connected to the topic of the unit part.

**Teaching tips**  Short tips on how to deal with a variety of problems that particularly German-speaking learners of English have, e.g. "false friends", and how to avoid them.

**(V) and (P)**  A (V) indicates vocabulary that may need to be pre-taught in order to complete the activity successfully, while a (P) indicates vocabulary that might present pronunciation difficulties for German native speakers.

**Photocopiables**  Each unit part provides one photocopiable activity or worksheet plus its recommended method and placement within the lesson. Answer keys for the photocopiables are provided at the back of the *Teaching Guide*.

## Make the most of your teaching skills

There are so many ways of teaching. Opportunities for utilizing many different teaching methods still exist, and it is in your hands to decide how to "get your message across". Regardless of your background and teaching experience, we'd like to suggest some Dos and Don'ts that you might want to consider.

### Preparing for lessons

**Do** make the best use of the room in which you are teaching, i.e. lighting, fresh air, curtains or blinds, heating and furnishings. Arrange the tables so that everyone can see everyone else all the time, e.g. in a horseshoe or "round table" formation. Seeing each other is vital because we all lip-read as we listen, which is particularly important when learning another language.

**Do** make sure you have everything you need for the lesson: coursebook, technology, photocopies, pens or chalk, and any additional extras such as dice or paper.

### Creating a comfortable atmosphere for all learners

**Do** regard your students as your partners and as a team.

**Do** encourage and promote cooperative learning.

**Do** use appropriate body language, i.e. make eye contact possible at all times without staring at students. Remain turned in their direction as much as you can and make sure they do the same, to you and to each other.

**Don't** "lecture" your students. Set a comfortable pace for talking and explaining to them while leaving sufficient space and opportunity for their reactions and replies. This may feel much longer to you than it does to them.

**Don't** talk too much or too little. It may be difficult, but be aware of traps such as feeling that a quiet pause must be filled with speech.

**Don't** move around too much or too often, but don't remain seated passively behind the desk either. Move about naturally; encourage movement on the part of the students while carrying out games or mobile activities.

**Do** keep in mind the physical abilities of your class while planning your lessons.

**Do** praise and encourage your class as a group as well as individual students, but avoid exaggerated or unnatural praise, as students may feel ridiculed.

**Do** offer some "inside information" about yourself now and then, e.g. about your own experience in learning another language, but aim to keep the students' speaking time at a maximum.

### General suggestions for carrying out activities

**Do** vary pairwork and group work as well as group sizes. This will produce a greater response and more information from the students, helping them to acquire and retain knowledge.

**Do** use blackboards or whiteboards and flipcharts. "Chalk and talk", i.e. putting words or ideas in writing in full view and then initiating a discussion about them is a method which, in moderation, functions well and is probably not familiar to the students, but is also an enormously important input channel for visual learners.

**Do** read out anything you write on a board or flipchart. In contrast to the visual learner type, hearing the target language is the most important input channel for auditive learners.

**Don't** limit the content of what your students want to talk about to what is in the book. Leave room for students to practise English even if they digress from the topic at hand.

### Preventing and correcting errors

**Do** pre-teach difficult or crucial lexical items where appropriate, i.e. in cases where vocabulary work is likely to become too time-consuming or, even worse, where lack of knowledge could lead to demotivation. As mentioned above, this *Teaching Guide* provides a selection of the most important new words and/or words that cause pronunciation problems with each exercise.

**Do** correct mistakes with care. Distinguish between systematic mistakes and slips of the tongue and decide whether you correct students immediately or collect errors and then go through these towards the end of the lesson. The trickiest aspect of correcting is running the risk of interrupting the flow of speaking.

### Encouraging learning outside of the classroom

**Do** encourage discovery and research by asking students to look for material at home, on the Internet, and in books, papers and magazines. Also make sure that you acknowledge their efforts and build the results into the following sessions.

## Using German in class

Encourage your students to use as little German in class as possible. Point out that being able to express yourself only using English is an important skill to acquire, especially if they use English in international contexts where German may not be understood. If they lack a particular word, they should practise rephrasing and explaining instead of simply using a German word. Illustrate the problem with a simple example, e.g. that a bartender in a pub will not understand "I would like to have a *Radler* (or *Alsterwasser*)." but will understand "beer mixed with a soft drink".
Invite students to bring their own dictionaries to class but also suggest they bring a monolingual dictionary instead of or in addition to a bilingual one.
If you encounter any personality conflicts in class, it is recommendable to sort things out in German to give students the opportunity to express themselves as clearly as possible. It is advisable to discuss such things either before or after class.

# Teaching the four classic skills

### Reading

The coursebook offers a wide range of different reading texts which illustrate the grammar concept as well as introduce new vocabulary. As all texts are designed to be as authentic as possible – presenting natural, idiomatic English – each text inevitably contains a number of unknown words, phrases and structures. Encourage students to read for gist first. This helps your students gain confidence in understanding what the text is about without understanding every word. Even though potentially difficult words have been noted in the *Teaching Guide*, read texts beforehand to check for additional words, especially those that are essential for understanding the gist of the text. Here are a few ideas for pre-teaching vocabulary:

– Use the words in context before students do a reading task. Explain the words as you go along.
– Write each word and its explanation on a card. Distribute a card to each student who then is "responsible" for that word. This can mean that you include a short activity in which a student either presents his or her word to the rest of the class, walks around the class and "teaches" the word to every other student, or simply says the word and swaps cards until every student has seen every word and description at least once.
– Write the words on the board and ask the class who knows any of them. As *A New Start* is a refresher course, some of your students may have heard one or two of the words before and can explain them to their fellow students.
– If appropriate, provide visuals. These can range from the actual objects to cut-out pictures or a photo that visualizes actions. This strategy could also be combined with the second suggestion above (words and explanations on cards). If you are good at miming, it may be fun to try to explain the meaning of some words and phrases this way.
– The least time-consuming way to introduce lexical items and their translations is to provide a list, with or without explanations, either on the board, on a separate handout or via some other media, and to go through the list as a class.

### Listening

Listening to the CD is very different from listening to the teacher or to the other students, where there is inevitably gesticulation and mimicry to assist understanding. It is a good idea to pre-teach difficult vocabulary (see the paragraph 'Reading' above for ideas) or to let the students look at the transcript after completing the tasks, maybe even reading it aloud themselves (particularly if it is a dialogue). With weaker learning groups you may also decide to let students read the text as they listen if you feel they will probably understand too little from listening alone.

Emphasize the enjoyment aspect of the listening texts in *Home study*. Recommend that the students listen to the CD in spare moments, when driving, doing the ironing, or simply relaxing in an armchair with a cup of tea.

### Speaking

There is a variety of speaking activities and tasks in the coursebook, including gap-fill activities, integrated skills tasks, thought-provoking or controversial questions and statements, ideas for guided discussions as well as for open discussions, questionnaires, role-plays and games.

Speaking in one's non-native language can be daunting, particularly for adult learners worried about making mistakes, but it can also bring a heady sense of achievement. Pairwork is less daunting for shy students, and gives maximum talking time to each student. Having students compare their answers in pairs first before going through the answers in class provides students an additional opportunity to speak.

Role-plays and questionnaires (note taking and reporting) are very useful for practising the questions and responses needed in everyday situations. Be encouraging, give positive feedback, and try to save corrections until afterwards unless mistakes greatly impair communication. Errors can be reviewed as a class at the completion of each activity, keeping anonymous who made which error.

The *Sound Check* activities in the coursebook focus on potential pronunciation and intonation difficulties. Some students learn particularly well through imitation. The *Class openers* described in this *Teaching Guide* help to break the ice in the group and personalize the lesson. It also helps students to switch their brains more easily into "English mode".

Personalization — i.e. letting the students relate the coursebook content to their individual experiences — is in general an important speaking stimulus. Ideas for questions to start off personalized discussions or to prompt the articulation of individual views are given throughout the coursebook.

Visual aids can also be the focus of a speaking activity: diagrams and flowcharts, for example, provide a framework which guides the speaker through a conversation or a presentation or provides some factual input to fuel a discussion.

Keep in mind that no one should ever be laughed at, regardless of what they say, but that laughing together can be a wonderful experience.

**Writing**

Writing is not a dominant part of the learning programme. However, each *Home study*, Part B promotes the writing of short texts. It will help the students if you correct (and, if required, assess) written work that they hand in. The homework suggestions in the *Teaching Guide* also offer additional alternatives for writing tasks. Emphasize to students that written tasks do not have to be long, but their aim is to consolidate what students have learned.

Encourage students to rewrite their texts after having received your feedback. It gives them the feeling of achievement and a language model to refer to, which is particularly useful when it comes to writing texts that require certain standard phrases, e.g. in business or private correspondence. When revising their work, students should look up unknown words in a dictionary and make use of the *Grammar and Vocabulary Booklet*.

In this introduction we have tried to stress the significance of fulfilment and enjoyment for the students as they progress through the course with your guidance. We hope that you gain satisfaction, pleasure and a positive teaching experience from working with this book. Enjoy your course with *A New Start Refresher A2*!

# Part A  Friends and relatives

| | |
|---|---|
| **Topics/Vocabulary** | Interests; family members |
| **Grammar** | *be, have got, can*; possessive determiners; possessive *'s* |
| **Functions** | Describing yourself, friends and family; asking about names |
| **Home study** | Questions and negatives with *be* and *have got*; possessive determiners; possessive *'s* |
| **Photocopiable** | Page 50 |
| **Extra materials** | **Class opener:** Thick pens or markers and cardboard or heavy paper; **2 Practice:** A5 or A6 paper (optional); **7 Let's Talk:** paper (A5 or larger) |

**Class opener**  Give each student a piece of cardboard or heavy paper and thick pens and ask them to write a name card to put on the table in front of them. During the lesson, collect the cards, shuffle and redistribute. Have students identify who their card belongs to.

**1** **FOCUS**  (V) *flat, married, neighbour, nurse*
Ask your students to look at the introductory question in **(1)** and say what they think. Write e.g. *I think they are brother and sister.* or just *brother and sister* on the board. Collect your students' ideas on the board, then proceed to **(2)**.

Ask students to look at the **Language Box** individually, then go through the forms together. You could add a table on the board containing the relevant personal pronouns and present forms of *to be*, i.e. *I – am / you – are / he, she, it – is / we, you, they – are*. As this is the first Language Box, draw your students' attention to the reference to the Grammar and Vocabulary Booklet and have them turn to the corresponding page. Point out that this is mainly for self-study purposes and that answer keys are provided. Give students a chance to ask questions in the subsequent class in case they had problems.

> Some students might find it helpful if you introduce grammatical terms such as *singular, plural*, etc. so they can acquire a framework of technical terms.

> Students may ask if *Has she got ...?* can also be expressed with *Does she have ...?* You can tell them that more simple present forms will be introduced in the next unit.

**2** **PRACTICE**  While your students are reading the instructions, hand out the A5/6 paper. Remind students that the papers will be collected. Tell them not to look at what the others are writing down, to keep things easy and to stick to the truth if they think it's not too personal. For a weak class, write some completed examples on the board (e.g. *I'm from Neukirchen. / I have two alligators. / My interests are animals and running.*) To continue, you could have students either read individual sentences and have the others guess as soon as they think they know who it is, or read all the information and then put it to a vote.

**3** **LET'S TALK**  **Optional photocopiable**  Especially in a weaker class, this supplemental activity can help students
 gain additional ideas and prepare for the Let's Talk tasks. Give a copy to each student. In pairs, they can fill in the table with the phrases. Check a few questions with the class to revise short answers (i.e. *Yes, I have. / No, I haven't.*).

After they've read the instructions to Let's Talk, ask your students to complete the two open sentences in **(1)**. Encourage the students to talk to as many different people as possible and to ask more questions, e.g. *Can you play the piano?* Remind them to take notes about names and answers. Have them report their findings to a partner as described in **(2)**. Then ask the class for the most interesting findings (e.g. *Nobody I talked to is a good swimmer.*) or do a class survey (e.g. *Who is a good swimmer? Hands up!*).

**4** **FOCUS**  (V) *fridge, cottage, researcher, exciting* (P) *daughter*
**1 02**  Carry out **(1)** as presented in the coursebook. Repeat the recording upon request.
For **(2)**, if you only played the audio once for **(1)**, ask students to read the conversation text before you play it a second time. If you've played the audio twice, it most likely won't be necessary to have your students read through the text before listening and filling the gaps.

Clarify vocabulary in **(2)** on demand. If students ask about family terms (e.g. *son-in-law*, *grandchildren*), you could discuss the words requested or tell them that there will be an activity dealing with that word family on the next page.

Look at the **Language Box** with your students. Ask them to find the second example of the 's possessive in the dialogue (*Tom: Are these Lucas and Maria's children?*) and think of some examples of their own which you can collect on the board. You could offer a table illustrating the different possible structures, e.g. *Tom's, Lucas and Maria's, Tom's and Irene's*.

> German native speakers often mix up the translations for the German *See* and *Meer*. As *sea* is in the dialogue, remind your students of the proper translations *lake* and *sea*.
> The correct translation for the German *Kinder kriegen* is another issue. Point out that the correct expression is *to have children*, not *to ~~get~~ children*.

**5** **SOUND CHECK**  **1 03**
Before the listening in **(1)**, encourage students to try saying the abbreviations aloud. After listening, practise saying the abbreviations again individually or in unison. A revision of the alphabet should be done prior to **(2)**. Introduce the phonetic script on p. 125 of the coursebook and ask students to find a "Germish" transcription of their own (e.g. *äi* for A, *sie* for C), or ask them to find a word in which the letter is pronounced the same as when spelled (e.g. *baby* for A, *Cindy* for C). This could be a pairwork activity which is followed by collecting all students' ideas on the board. Then carry out **(2)** as described in the coursebook.

**6** **TUNE IN**  **1 04**
After doing the activity as described in the coursebook, check the results with the class by asking some students to spell the names of Tom's friends. As a follow-up activity, ask students to spell their names and/or two difficult names in small groups or in pairs.

> A common question is how to deal with the German umlaut. Explain that you can say *a/o/u umlaut* for the German *ä/ö/ü*.

**7** **LET'S TALK**
Tell students to read the instructions and vocabulary in **(1)**. Before they turn to the pairwork, you could ask the class for two or three examples which you can collect on the board. Carry out **(2)** and **(3)** as presented in the coursebook.

> Some people might not want to talk about their own families and could instead use a family from a soap opera or a family they know or make up.

> German native speakers often make three mistakes when talking about people in their family trees: (a) *Sie ist verheiratet mit.* = She is married ~~with~~ to ... (b) He is ~~a~~ single. (c) He is **a** doctor.

**Homework suggestion** Ask students to draw a more comprehensive version of a family tree or make a poster, even including pictures, and to write a few sentences about it.

**HOME STUDY**
Encourage students to complete the Home study before the next class. Remind them that the keys are in the coursebook.

### Keys for Unit 1 – Part A

**1.2** 1 D I 2 C I 3 A I 4 E I 5 B

**4.1** 1 Jen I 2 James I 3 Tristan I 4 Becca I 5 Maria I 6 Ollie I 7 Lucas I 8 Beth

**4.2** 1 your I 2 my I 3 his I 4 her I 5 Our I 6 my I 7 your I 8 their

**5.2** Digital Versatile Disk I Federal Bureau of Investigation I International Business Machines I Personal Computer I

Global Positioning System I Very Important Person I United Nations I Cable News Network I Member of Parliament I World Health Organization I British Broadcasting Corporation I Disc Jockey I Bed and Breakfast

**6** Nicole Mollet; Tereza Kadlec; Jürg/Juerg Propicjek

| Topics/Vocabulary | Furniture; places in a town; holiday cottages; English tours from Erding |
|---|---|
| **Grammar** | *there is/are*; *some/any*; prepositions |
| **Functions** | Describing your house/flat/town |
| **Home study** | Living in the West Country |
| **Photocopiable** | Page 51 |
| **Extra materials** | **2 Let's Talk:** A4 paper, optionally pencils, rubbers/erasers and tape |

**Class opener**  Begin by asking what your students remember about their classmates.

**1  FOCUS**  (V) *dining room, curtains, blinds, armchair, favourite, bookcase, fish tank, cosy, comfortable, plants*
(P) *comfortable*
Ask your students to look at the instructions and pictures in **(1)**. With the whole group, tell them to say aloud any English words they know. If they don't know a word, encourage them to describe the item in English and avoid using German vocabulary. Aim for at least a dozen words. Pairwork is also possible. Students can then read the texts for **(2)** individually and compare answers with the class.

Go through each section of the **Language Box**. For each section, ask your students to come up with examples of their own and collect them on the board. Remind them to look at the Grammar and Vocabulary Booklet for more explanations and activities.

Round off the activity by having the class discuss **(3)** in small groups and report back to the class.

**2  LET'S TALK**  For **(1)**, hand out the A4 sheets, pencils and rubbers/erasers. To prevent students from looking at each other's drawings, ask them to sit back-to-back while giving the descriptions. When you see that students have completed the drawings, direct them to **(2)**. If possible, you could collect the drawings on the board and then have your students vote for the nicest room, best artwork, etc.

**3  PRACTICE**  (V) *cooker, fitted wardrobe, coat hooks, hall*
Ask your students to either complete the gap text together or first do the gap text on their own and compare answers afterwards.

Students often confuse *in der Nähe von = near* and *in der Nähe = nearby*. Point out the difference and ask your students for some examples which you can collect on the board.

**4  TUNE IN**  Ensure that students read the list of words before playing the audio.
1 05

**5  LET'S TALK**  Introduce the File pages in the coursebook. When assigning the pairwork in **(1)**, tell your students not to look at their partner's page, but to get the missing information by asking questions. After the partner activity has been completed, ask the class which of the villages they would like to live in most, comparing the villages as modelled in the coursebook. Then carry out **(2)** as presented.

To extend the activity, divide your class into small groups. Each group should consist of people who live in different villages, towns, or districts, etc. In their groups, students then compare the different places. Encourage them to think of businesses or places other than the ones in the book. Finally, ask them to report their findings to the class.

Read the **Culture Tip** together and ask the students to compare the information provided to their supermarkets.

**6  OUT AND ABOUT**  (V) *accommodation, hot tub, quiet, coastal walks, historical sights, renovated, stony, castle, expensive*
Introduce the activity by asking students about their experience with booking online, e.g. *Do you book your holidays online? Are there any websites you know?* Now ask them to read the scenario and instructions in **(1)**. After clarifying vocabulary, ask the students to discuss the question in pairs and then report back to the class.
1 06

Proceed with **(2)** as presented in the coursebook, then compare answers with the class.

> Before dividing your class for **(3)**, revise suitable structures. Point out that your students should focus on the *Is/Are there* structure. A common mistake is *Has it a TV?* instead of *Is there a TV?* Have them read the audio transcript on p. 99 of the coursebook and underline examples.

For **(3)**, divide the class into holiday-makers and travel agents and have them read the respective instructions. The website graphic on p. 12 should serve as a guide for both roles. Ask holiday-makers to note the things they want and/or need and who they want to travel with; the travel agents should note the kind of accommodation they have on offer and other details. Now ask the travel agents to sit down in their "offices". The holiday-makers then approach the different agents to find the best accommodation for their needs. In a weak class you could provide some useful phrases for the dialogues on the board. Finally, ask your class who made a successful deal with whom.

**Optional photocopiable** This activity aims to revise *There is/isn't ... / There are/aren't ...*, prepositions of location, and furniture vocabulary. Either or both steps can be completed.
**Step 1** Cut the photocopied worksheets horizontally. For each pair, hand out one copy of the picture of Room 1, placing it face down on the desk. Until you give the signal, the copy should stay face down. Before giving the signal, tell the students they will have one minute to look at the picture. The goal is for them to remember the objects in the room and their positions. After the minute is over, have the students turn the picture face down again. Ask each pair to make a list of what they saw. After a few minutes, review the lists with the class.
**Step 2** Hand out the picture of Room 2 (or, if Step 1 is skipped, the full A4 page). In pairs, students should compare and contrast the pictures using the target phrases, prepositions and vocabulary.

**7**  Prior to playing the audio, ensure that students understand the vocabulary in the instructions and questions.

 To prepare students for the Home study, see if a student can introduce the concept of a "word spider". On the board, draw a word spider that revises vocabulary from the unit (e.g. businesses in a village or objects in a living room), and collect ideas. Alternatively, have the students work in pairs.

**Keys for Unit 1 – Part B**

**1.2** Tom has only got two chairs, but he says he has got three. Irene says most of her plants are in front of the window, but they're not.

**3** 1 aren't any | 2 are some | 3 are some | 4 is a | 5 is a | 6 isn't a | 7 is a | 8 aren't any

**4** Tick: *bakery, bank, chemist's, newsagent's, pub, supermarket*

| 5.1 village | church | bookshop | pub | bank | supermarket |
|---|---|---|---|---|---|
| Ashford | no | no | 4 | no | yes |
| Compton | no | no | 2 | no | no |
| Beckbridge | yes | 2 | 3 | yes | yes |
| Daggerby | yes | yes | 8 | yes | yes |

**6.2** *3 or 4 rooms* | Tick: ** £200 – £400, *** £400 – £600 | Tick: *garden, in a quiet village, by the sea, near sandy beaches, near historical sights, near pubs and restaurants, horse-riding and fishing*

**7** 1 She was an English teacher and he was a coach driver. He drove her and her class on a trip to Great Britain. | 2 They complain about the small rooms and the cleanliness of the bathrooms. | 3 It's the cheapest accommodation and you can practise your English. | 4 The owners of the B&B they were staying at. | 5 London

| Topics/Vocabulary | Attitudes towards cooking and food; household tasks |
|---|---|
| **Grammar** | Simple present; adverbs of frequency |
| **Functions** | Asking for and giving information; telling the time |
| **Home study** | Questions and negatives; word order; vocabulary work |
| **Photocopiable** | Page 52 |
| **Extra materials** | None |

**Class opener** Start the class by giving students the opportunity to read aloud their paragraphs from C Writing from the Home study in Unit 1 Part B. Bring a short sample you've written in case no one wants to volunteer. Challenge students to think of questions to ask the reader that revise the vocabulary as well as the *has (it) got* and *is there / are there* question structures from Unit 1.

**1** **FOCUS** | `1 09`

(V) *added sugar, plate, tasty*

Ask the students the questions in **(1)** as a class or have them work in pairs. Answers could be tallied on the board. Before beginning **(2)**, it might be helpful to make sure that students know the vocabulary used to name the different countries in the audio (*Holland = Dutch, Britain = British, the States = American*).

Move on to **(2)** and carry out the activity as presented in the coursebook. Check the answers before proceeding to **(3)**.

Carry out **(4)** using pairwork as indicated. Use the **Language Box** to explain the simple present for statements. Illustrate the concept further by listing several simple sentences on the board. Then make the sentences negative, pointing out the use of *don't/doesn't* and the infinitive. In the same manner, review question formation. Be sure to draw special attention to the *-s* needed for the third person.

**2** **PRACTICE**

(P) *oil*

Give students a few minutes to form the questions prior to the pairwork.

**3** **LET'S TALK**

(V) *to go out for a meal / to go for a meal out, frozen food, organic*

> To review question formation with question words, draw a chart with the following columns: *question word, do/don't/does/doesn't, subject, infinitive,* and *other information*. Ask students to come up to the board and write their own questions in the simple present. To prepare for the next activity, illustrate what happens when *how many/much, what type of,* and *what kind of* start the sentence, i.e. they are sometimes followed by an object, and elicit corresponding examples from the students.

Use 3 Let's Talk to encourage students to start a conversation with their partner. You could make a competition out of it to see who can have the longest conversation by timing the conversations or by seeing who is still talking after a specified length of time.

**4** **LET'S TALK**

Prior to dividing the class into groups, give students time to form the questions they will need for this activity. The questions could then be checked in class. For **(1)**, students should begin with the topic from the list that interests them most and make brief notes as needed in order to prepare for **(2)**. Encourage a contribution from every class participant for **(2)**.

**5** **TUNE IN** | `1 10`

Carry out **(1)** as presented in the coursebook. Point out that they might know some other ways to say the same times, e.g. *It's a quarter past three / quarter after three* (American English) / *three fifteen; twenty past four / twenty after four; half past three / three thirty; ten to five / ten till five / ten before five* (American English). Point out that the 24-hour clock is only used for transport timetables and for the military. Direct students to do **(2)** as described in the coursebook.

**6** **LET'S TALK**

Ask the students to write out the questions needed to elicit answers for each statement. Then encourage them to get up and mingle with other students until they have found someone who matches each statement in the coursebook. Remind students to use an *-s* with the third person when they write notes or report their findings to the class, e.g. *Clara gets up at 6 o'clock.* as Clara will actually say *I get up at 6 o'clock.*

**7** **FOCUS** (V) *noise, vacuum, dust, shelves* (P) *vacuum*

 Proceed with **(1)** as presented in the coursebook. You could point out that frequency adverbs can be stressed in order to add emphasis. If a pair of students is asked to read the dialogue aloud to check the answers, the speakers could also try to stress the frequency adverbs to make the reading more authentic. Students work individually for **(2)**.

 To help students build their vocabularies, ask for collocations used for household tasks and list them on the board. As an alternative, have students first identify and underline the collocations in the transcript.

Before or after going over the **Language Box**, refer the students to the statements in **(2)** again. These sentences provide additional examples to those in the Language Box.
To consolidate both the collocations and the frequency adverbs, you could ask the students if they have had problems similar to the ones in **(1)** at home or in their workplaces.

**8** **PRACTICE** Point out that **(1)** and **(2)** refer to students' pairwork partners and not their partners in their private lives. Then have students complete **(1)** and encourage discussion. Walk around and make a note of any mistakes; review them after **(2)** with the whole class. For **(2)**, students report their findings to the class. Remind them to use *-s* for the third person singular.

**Optional photocopiable** Hand out a copy to each student. Students can tick the boxes for themselves and put their names in the top corner. Collect the papers and read out each one, e.g. *This person doesn't love Indian food, but always drives carefully.* Students should guess which paper belongs to whom. If the class is large, divide the students into two groups.

**HOME STUDY** Remind students to revise what they have learned by completing the Home study and by checking their answers in the coursebook.

**Homework suggestion** To expand on the Lerntipp, students could test their memories by collecting their post-its after a week, putting them aside for a while and then trying to post them around the house again. To review what's been covered in Unit 2 Part A, students could write questions and answers related to activities or tasks that are carried out in a particular room and post them on the respective doors, e.g. on the kitchen door: *What do I eat for breakfast? I usually eat cornflakes and toast. / Does my husband clean the kitchen? No, he doesn't. He sometimes cleans the bathroom.*

**Keys for Unit 2 – Part A**

**1.2** Mark = Dutch ı Bill = American ı
Sara = British

**1.3** 1 Bill and Mark ı 2 Sara ı 3 Sara ı 4 Mark ı
5 Sara and Bill

**Language Box** don't/doesn't ı do/does

**2** 2 Does Mark go to the States on business?
Yes, he does. He always eats too much. ı
3 Do Italians cook with a lot of oil? Yes, they
do, but they cook with good olive oil. ı
4 Does Sara eat German crisps? No, she
doesn't. She thinks they're boring. ı 5 Does
Mark like burgers and chips? Yes, he does.

He thinks fast food restaurants are great. ı
6 Do Italian restaurants stay open all day?
No, they don't. They all shut between
2 and 7.

**5.1** 1 D ı 2 C ı 3 F ı 4 E ı 5 B ı 6 A

**Language Box** before ı after

**7.1** 1 always ı 2 never ı 3 often ı 4 usually ı
5 hardly ever ı 6 normally ı 7 usually ı
8 always ı 9 always ı 10 sometimes ı
11 often ı 12 always

**7.2** 1 F ı 2 F ı 3 F ı 4 T ı 5 F ı 6 T

| Topics/Vocabulary | Getting to know the British; London |
| --- | --- |
| **Grammar** | Adjectives and adverbs |
| **Functions** | Describing people; asking for directions |
| **Home study** | Special events in London |
| **Photocopiable** | Page 53 |
| **Extra materials** | None |

**Class opener** To revise the simple present, ask students what they know about food in other countries, e.g. *Hungarians use a lot of garlic. Italians eat pasta.* Make a list or chart on the board. As the topic in Part B is centered on Britain, be sure to include Britain, even if you have to provide the examples. It might be necessary to help students with vocabulary about food, e.g. *dish/Gericht, vegetable/Gemüse, spicy/scharf.* To transition to the topic in Part B, you could say *Now we know a little about what people in different countries eat. Let's take a look at some typical behaviour in Britain.*

**1**  **FOCUS** (V) *polite, queue, patiently, accidentally, to bump into (s.o./s.th.), to apologize, to shout at (s.o.), health, cheerfully, complain, manners, carelessly, trolley* (P) *queue, to apologize*
Have students answer the questions in **(1)** individually and then read the text. Do a quick survey of the class to find out how many people got all three questions correct.

Explain the difference between adjectives and adverbs by writing a pair of sentences on the board, e.g. *Tom speaks perfect English. Tom speaks English perfectly.* Ask students to translate the two example sentences into German to remind them of the difference between the two languages. Point out that verbs such as *to be, to feel, to look* and *to seem* require adjective forms and that some adverbs are irregular as well: *fast – fast, hard – hard, late – late,* and those which end in *-y.* Now draw the students' attention to the **Language Box** and ask them to read through the information and answer the multiple choice question.

> ! List the irregular adjectives and their adverbs in one corner of the board and leave the list up during the lesson.

Direct students to carry out **(2)** as described in the coursebook. Review the answers with the class. In **(3)**, encourage students to put their thoughts into sentences using adjectives and adverbs.

**2**  **PRACTICE** In this activity, students could answer the multiple choice questions either individually or in pairs. Check the answers with the class.

> ! Revise question formation and the position of adverbs in questions by choosing a student and asking a question such as *Do you normally eat slowly?* (It might be helpful to put a model sentence on the board showing the placement of the adverb.) Elicit short answers: *Yes, I do.* or *No, I don't.* The student then has to turn to the next student and ask another question that uses *always/normally/sometimes/often* plus an adverb; continue around the class so that every student has a chance to answer and ask a question.

**3** **PRACTICE** (V) *rude, sensible, sociable, miserable* (P) *sociable, miserable*
Give students time to fill in the gaps individually or with a partner. Round off the activity by collecting additional adjectives which describe personalities on the board.

**4** **LET'S TALK** Direct the students to do the activity as presented in the coursebook. Encourage them to get up and mingle so they can talk to as many of their classmates as possible. You could then ask the students to share their most interesting findings with the class.

**5** **PRACTICE** Carry out **(1)** as presented in the coursebook, checking the answers with the class.

> !  As it often causes confusion, and since the students had *hardly ever* in Part A of this unit, illustrate the difference between *hard* and *hardly*, i.e. *I work hard.* v. *I hardly (ever) work.*

After **(2)**, ask your students to take three of their adverb-verb combinations or three from the table in **(1)** and make a sentence with each. The same could be done for the adjective-noun combinations from **(2)**. Check for correct word order as the students are working or as a group afterwards.

**6** OUT AND ABOUT

(V) *capital, underground, to be in a hurry* (P) *Swedes, icon, arrogant*
Before moving to **(1)**, draw a mind map on the board starting with *LONDON* and ask students what they already know about the place. Alternatively, ask them to come up and write their ideas on the board. In either case, leave space for adjectives from the text, which can be collected either directly after **(1)** or later on as revision. Have students read the text and answer the questions in **(2)** either as a class or, if possible, in small groups made up of people who have different hometowns.

To extend Question 2 in **(2)**, encourage discussion within the small groups about the students' hometowns by putting some ideas on the board, e.g. *eating out, points of interest, public transport, shops, banks*. Then ask students to read the **Culture Tip**. Round off the activity by asking students to think of tips or advice for someone who is visiting their respective hometowns.

**7** OUT AND ABOUT

Before beginning **(1)** and **(2)**, point out that the verb *to take* is often used in two different ways when talking about transportation: one can *take the underground/bus/train*, etc. in the sense of *travel with (fahren mit / nehmen)*, or one can ask *How long does it take?* to refer to a length of time in the sense of *need (brauchen/dauern)*. Proceed with **(1)** and **(2)** as presented in the coursebook.

**Optional photocopiable** Distribute one copy to each student. Students first look at the map of London to help them see where the different landmarks are located. Students should then complete the names with the words provided. Then ask if they know any other places in London and have them mark the locations on the map.

**Homework suggestion** Students could find or draw a map of their hometowns, however big or small, marking any points of interest. Suggest that they bring their maps to the next lesson and give them the opportunity to briefly present them to the class or if everyone has done the assignment, to a partner.

HOME STUDY

Encourage the students to read the texts at home to learn more about London. Point out that the more difficult words have been underlined for them to translate. Remind them of the importance of writing in English to support what they've learned.

**Keys for Unit 2 – Part B**

**1.1** 1 b ǀ 2 a ǀ 3 b

**1.2 Adjectives:** first, true, interested, same, bad, terrible, fine, patient, famous, unhappy, polite, apologetic, sorry, first, good, important, careless, polite ǀ
**Adverbs:** truthfully, cheerfully, patiently, loudly, carelessly

**Language Box** adjective

**2** 1 carefully ǀ 2 polite ǀ 3 hard ǀ 4 well ǀ 5 bad

**3** 1 funny ǀ 2 serious ǀ 3 untidy ǀ 4 cheerful ǀ 5 sociable ǀ 6 rude ǀ 7 sensible ǀ 8 shy

**5.1 work:** quickly, late, quietly, badly, well, hard ǀ **play:** quietly, badly, well, hard ǀ **drive:** quickly, badly, well, dangerously ǀ **speak:** quickly, quietly, badly, well ǀ **arrive:** late, quietly, early ǀ **get up:** quickly, late, quietly, early ǀ **leave:** quickly, late, early, quietly ǀ **come:** quickly, late, early

**7.1** 1 Covent Garden ǀ 2 Piccadilly Line ǀ 3 10 minutes

| Topics/Vocabulary | Free-time activities and hobbies |
|---|---|
| Grammar | Present progressive (present and future); present progressive and simple present |
| Functions | Talking about things you are doing/plan to do |
| Home study | Present progressive (present and future); questions in the present |
| Photocopiable | Page 54 |
| Extra materials | None |

**Class opener**  To introduce the topic of free time as well as to revise Unit 2 Part A (the language used to talk about time and the correct usage of frequency adverbs), ask the students to describe their daily or weekly schedules to a partner. You might want to give them a few minutes to write down a few ideas. In their schedules they should point out when they have free time. Take a class poll to see if students are happy with the amount of free time they have during a typical week. Note: Limit the discussion to schedules, as they will talk about their free time activities later in this unit.

> When talking about their schedules, students may need help with some collocations, e.g. *to wake/get up, to take a shower.*

**1  FOCUS**  (V) *to sled(ge), to walk the dog*

Ask your students to read the instructions to **(1)** and look at the top left picture. As most students will not know the vocabulary to describe the photo, write *Two people are sledging.* on the board and invite students to say more about this picture, e.g. *They are wearing winter clothes./They are smiling/having a good time.* and write their suggestions on the board to clarify the *to be + verb + ing* structure of the present progressive. Now ask the class to talk about the other pictures with a partner. Help with vocabulary and correct grammar mistakes. After a few minutes, ask students to share some of their ideas with the class.

After students have read the instructions and looked at the word spiders in **(2)**, ask them to use some of the examples to make sentences, ideally including frequency adverbs, e.g. *sometimes, often.* Give them time to add their ideas and then talk with a partner. You could then collect some ideas on the board before directing the students to **(3)**. Round off the activity by asking students to report back their most interesting findings to the class.

> During 1 Focus, students may ask you about details concerning the differences between the simple present and present progressive. Either explain the details here or give them the basic information relevant for this activity and tell them that further details will follow in 3 Focus.

**2  PRACTICE**  For **(1)**, have students work in pairs or small groups. Prior to beginning, explain that there isn't only one correct answer. After a few minutes, have students report their ideas. Collect them on the board and vote on the best or most original ideas. Then move on to **(2)** as presented in the coursebook. If some students cannot guess what their partner is miming, you can invite them to mime the activity for the rest of the class and see if other students can figure it out.

**Optional photocopiable**  To further practise describing activities, divide the class into small groups or pairs. Hand out a copy of p.54 and a set of cut-out cards to each team. Students take turns picking up one of the cards and reading it aloud. Their partner(s) find the matching picture and place the card beneath it.

**3  FOCUS**  1 14  (V) *advanced*

Start as presented in the coursebook. You can check students' answers by asking two volunteers to read the dialogue. Then work through the **Language Box**. After students have read it through and ticked the boxes, ask them to find more examples of the two tenses in the transcript. Check their suggestions and then ask students for some more examples of their own to consolidate.

**4** `PRACTICE` **(V) and (P)** *autumn (fall in American English)*
Carry on as presented in the coursebook. You could extend the activity by asking students to talk about things they usually do at the weekends, on certain days of the week, etc. Ask your class to report back the most interesting findings.

**5** `FOCUS` **(V)** *human resources, as a matter of fact, you're kidding*
`1 15` After students have read the instructions to **(1)**, refer them to the **Language Box**. Explain that they will hear the two different uses of the present progressive in the dialogue, then play the recording. Ask the class to read the dialogue again and individually mark the forms as presented in the instructions to **(2)**. Before reviewing the answers with the group, have students compare their answers with a partner. Upon completing **(3)**, ask students to report back to the class.

**6** `PRACTICE` Prior to **(1)**, assign new partners. Ask the students to read the instructions and the example sentences on the page. Then ask one student of each pair to turn to the File page. Explain that they need to form questions so that their partner will answer with the missing information. Encourage the class not to peek at each other's tables! Check quickly as a group before turning to **(2)**. Tell students to fill in the table individually first. To illustrate the idea you could write some examples on the board, explaining that the first line is about themselves and the second line is about their pairwork partner. Completing the table in **(2)** might take longer than expected; give the class some time to fill in their ideas before they start to exchange information.

**Homework suggestion** As an additional homework assignment, you could invite students to bring along a photo or an advertisement to the next class, and show and describe it to their fellow students. To practise writing as well as the present progressive, they can also write down the description.

**HOME STUDY** Encourage students to extend the activities on the Home study page with examples of their own, e.g. *My daughter is playing with our dog. / My husband normally cycles to the station, but today it's raining too hard.*

**Keys for Unit 3 – Part A**

**2.1** **1** sending an email **2** writing a letter **3** cooking **4** watching TV **5** talking to a friend

**Language Box** present **regular**

**3** **1** at the moment **2** every **3** this term **4** usually

**5.2** Underline: I'm meeting; Are you doing; I'm leaving; Are you going; are you coming; I'm going; are you going; we're spending; we're visiting (Circle): after class; tomorrow night; tomorrow; when; at the end of next week; this weekend

**6.1**

|  | usually on Fridays | this Friday | usually on Saturdays | this Saturday |
|---|---|---|---|---|
| **Sarah** | go to the cinema | go to the theatre | do yoga | go for a walk |
| **Stephen** | watch TV | visit friends | go to the pub | go on a date |
| **Caroline** | do aerobics | do ballet | go shopping | go to London |
| **Laura** | go to a disco | go dancing | go swimming | visit grandmother |

| | |
|---|---|
| **Topics/Vocabulary** | Everyday activities; English radio in Germany; an American journalist in Berlin |
| **Grammar** | *love*, *hate*, *like*, etc. + *-ing* form; relative clauses |
| **Functions** | Expressing preferences; describing people/activities (with relative clauses) |
| **Home study** | Geocaching |
| **Photocopiable** | Page 55 |
| **Extra materials** | **5 Let's Talk:** A3 paper (if not available, A4); optionally, material to stick the paper to the wall, board, etc. |

**Class opener** Begin by writing a statement about one of your students on the board, e.g. *Chris usually plays cricket on Fridays.* You could use something they mentioned in 6 Practice of Part A or make something up. Ask the class whether the statement is true. Then ask the student, in this case Chris, if the class was right. Repeat with some more examples, then transition to 1 Focus by using the new structure, e.g. *Chris likes playing cricket. Let's see what Alex and Rachel like.*

**1**  **FOCUS**    (V) *develop, recipes, leisure-time activity* (P) *recipe, leisure*

 Have the students read the instructions to **(1)** and then fill in the gaps. Before playing the recording, give students some time to exchange answers with a partner. After playing the recording, draw the students' attention to the doubling of the consonant required for "jog". After going over the **Language Box**, remind your students of the third person *-s* and the *don't/doesn't* rules of the simple present.

Once students have read the instructions to **(2)**, offer them the option of taking notes. It might be necessary to help out with vocabulary. After students talk with a partner as described in **(2)**, you could ask them to share one fact about their partner with the class.

To get your class to move around a bit and to talk to different partners, ask them to get up and mingle and exchange one or two points with several classmates. After a few minutes, ask the students to report their most unusual findings to the group.

 **Optional photocopiable** Explain that the class is about to do a survey about the likes and dislikes of their fellow students. Give one part of the photocopiable to each student and clarify the structure by writing *What do you think about ironing?* and the possible answers *I like/love ironing.* and *I hate ironing.* on the board. Then ask the students to think of activities to add to the empty lines. Now tell the class to talk to as many of their fellow students as possible and ask each of them all the questions. After a few minutes, collect the results of the survey on the board.

**2** **SOUND CHECK**    Ask your students to read the instructions and look at the words and symbols. To clarify, you can write an example on the board for each stress pattern, using vocabulary from past units, e.g. *brother* for Oo or *holiday* for Ooo. Before playing the recording you can ask your class to look at the examples in pairs and tick the boxes with a pencil. Then play the recording and check as a group by asking different students to read out the words.

**3** **PRACTICE**    (P) *athlete, colleague*

Before turning to this activity you can ask your class if they have ever heard of relative clauses and invite those who have to give an example which you can collect on the board. With or without this pre-activity, tell your students that they will learn how to combine sentences about the two people in 1 Focus, Rachel and Alex. First turn to the **Language Box** and introduce the relative clause structure. Proceed with 3 Practice as presented in the coursebook with students working either individually or with a partner. If working individually, students could compare their answers with a partner before reviewing them with the class.

**4** LET'S TALK (V) *chef, lawyer* (P) *lawyer*

Tell the class to first read the instructions to **(1)** and then match the pictures and jobs on their own. Before having the students turn to their classmates for **(2)**, point out the correct structures using the examples under the instruction line. Tell them that they will have to report back to the class at the end of **(2)** and give the reasons for their choices. In a weaker class, you could write e.g. *The woman who is cutting vegetables on page 28 is Rachel.* on the board to further illustrate the structure. Proceed to **(3)** as a complete group.

Students often confuse the English *chef* with the German *Chef (= boss)*. Another common mistake is the translation *chief* for the German *Chef*.

**5** LET'S TALK (V) *healthy, questionnaire, exercise* (P) *questionnaire*

Have students complete the table in **(1)** and compare with a partner. Before moving to **(2)**, do a poll to find out who is the healthiest. Important: The questionnaire and discussion should focus on the lighter side and not be used for putting down smokers or couch potatoes.

For **(2)**, provide two blank A3 sheets to each pair and ask them to collect their ideas on the two different pages, one for healthy things and one for unhealthy things. Tell the class that their ideas will be put up on the board or wall. As required, assist with vocabulary. After a few minutes, ask the students to put their sheets on the board. Invite the class to look at all the ideas and comment on them. You can round off the activity by asking the pairs which of the suggestions they actually do themselves.

**6** OUT AND ABOUT (V) *improving, Forces, phone-ins, available* (P) *digital*

Introduce the activity by asking students if they have ever listened to any English-speaking radio stations, either in Germany or abroad. Then ask them to read the list in **(1)**. Before turning to **(2)**, ask the class if they know any of the suggestions listed. For **(2)**, divide your class into small groups, then proceed as presented. Round off the activity by comparing answers as a class.

**7** ENGLISH NEAR ME
1 18

Find out if anyone in the class has heard of Anouschka Pearlman before and invite them to say what they know about her. Then turn to the instructions and proceed as presented in the coursebook. After comparing the answers, you can end the activity by asking students which radio presenters they know and what they like – or don't like – about them.

**Homework suggestion** As an additional optional homework assignment, you can invite students to try out the radio stations and/or websites suggested in the coursebook or by other students. In the following lessons they can present their impressions, e.g. interesting things they heard or found out, how easy or hard it was to understand the presenters.

HOME STUDY

As an additional homework assignment, you could invite students to prepare example sentences using the words they learned in B Vocabulary.

**Keys for Unit 3 – Part B**

**1.1** 1 inviting | 2 cooking | 3 going | 4 reading | 5 doing | 6 jogging | 7 swimming | 8 cycling

**2** oO enjoy | Oo dinner, jogging , brilliant | oOo develop, tomorrow | Ooo bicycle | oOoo activity

**Language Box** who/that | which/that

**3** 1 who/that; D | 2 which/that; C | 3 which/that; A | 4 who/that; E | 5 which/that; B

**7** 1 T | 2 F | 3 F | 4 T | 5 T | 6 F

| Topics/Vocabulary | Budget airlines; air travel |
|---|---|
| **Grammar** | *was/were*; simple past (regular verbs) |
| **Functions** | Comparing past and present; talking about the past |
| **Home study** | Simple past; word order; vocabulary work |
| **Photocopiable** | Page 56 |
| **Extra materials** | **7 Let's Talk:** Copies of the mind map on p. 34 in the coursebook (optional); **9 Let's Talk:** Dice, game pieces and the cut-out culture & problem cards |

**Class opener**  If you introduced the additional homework at the end of Unit 3, invite students to present what they have prepared. To transition to the topic of the unit and revise the grammar in Unit 3, draw a timeline on the board that covers the next 12 months and ask *Who is flying somewhere for their next holiday? / When are you going?* and add the information to the timeline. Once you've identified whose trip will take place first, see if the class can form a few more questions for their classmate using the present progressive, e.g. *Where are you staying?*

**1**  **FOCUS**  **1 20**  (V) *budget airline, advantage, disadvantage, opinion, rich, experience, seat, rush, ordinary*

To begin **(1)**, ask your students to look at the picture and then collect the names of the budget airlines they mention on the board. After reading the instructions for **(2)**, students could first brainstorm in pairs. Write *advantages* and *disadvantages* on the board in two columns. After two to three minutes, collect the students' ideas on the board.

Carry out **(3)** as presented in the coursebook. For **(4)**, take a quick poll to find out which opinions your students agree with. For the second question, divide the class into small groups to provide enough speaking time. Round off the activity by asking the class to report back the most interesting stories.

Be lenient when it comes to correcting tense mistakes. The past tense is reintroduced in this unit.

**2**  **PRACTICE**  (V) *rise*

Before turning to the writing activity, look at the **Language Box** together. Point out that *there was/were* stands for both the German *da war/waren* and *es gab*, just like the present forms on p. 10 in the coursebook. Before students start writing the sentences individually, you can suggest alternatives like *…years ago* for *in the past*. Once the students have finished, compare as a class.

Students often want to use a direct translation for the German phrase *vor fünf Jahren*, or *five years ago* in English. Point this out before they begin writing, or be prepared to correct this error should it arise.

*Free* is often misinterpreted as *frei*, i.e. *available*. Explain that confusion may arise when someone asks for *free tickets* or *free seats* and introduce phrases such as *Are there any tickets available?* or *Is this seat taken?*

**3**  **LET'S TALK**  Complete this activity as presented in the coursebook. Invite students to add any additional ideas of their own. After a few minutes, ask them to present their ideas to the class. You could extend this activity by offering e.g. *What do you think about these changes?* or similar questions. Encourage your class to find positive aspects of any changes they discuss.

**4**  **FOCUS**  (V) *to arrange, to move, to water plants*

Students first fill in the gaps individually, then compare with a partner. As a class, look at the **Language Box** and ask the students for suggestions for the gaps. In a weaker class you could refer students to the Language Box before they do the gap fill.

Frequently, problems arise with negative forms and questions as students mix tenses, such as *don't realized*. A quick extra activity is to write two to three sentences such as *I met my sister.* on the board and ask students to provide the negative and question forms before you turn to 5 Practice.

**5**  **PRACTICE**  (V) *to feed*

Proceed as presented in the coursebook, then compare as a class.

**6**  **SOUND CHECK** ⏏ 1 21   Carry out as presented in the coursebook. Round off the activity by asking students to read out the words they put in the different columns.

**7** **LET'S TALK**   (V) *to share, to belong, memories, worst subject*

Ask your class to read the instructions, verbs and ideas. In a weaker class, you could collect more questions connected to the examples in the mind map (e.g. *Who/What was your favourite ...*, *What TV programmes did you ...)* before you divide them into pairs. Encourage the students to add their own aspects. Finish by inviting the class to share what they have found out about each other.

As an alternative, you can ask students to first expand the mind map before commencing their dialogues. To make this easier for the students, give them copies of the mind map on p. 32.

 Students often forget the *-ing* form after *like, hate* or *prefer*. To remind your students, you can refer them to p. 26 in the coursebook and point out that the *-ing* form also follows the past tense form of these verbs.

**8** **TUNE IN**   (V) *check in luggage, on time, departure gate, baggage reclaim area, lost luggage form*

⏏ 1 22   Go through **(1)** as presented in the coursebook. Focus on the proper use of the past tense. Concerning content, any retelling of the story that uses the correct order and covers the main points should be accepted. Stories such as those asked for in **(2)** are usually interesting for the whole group. Do this activity in small groups to provide enough talking time for each student.

**Optional photocopiable**

(V) *accommodation, exhibitions, What a shame!*

Divide the class into pairs and give each student a copy of the questionnaire. In turns, students now ask each other the questions and write their own and their partner's points in the boxes provided – the number of points given on the right for a *yes*, 0 points for a *no*. Point out that they should answer with *Yes, I/we did.* or *No, I/we didn't.* After completing the questionnaire, students add up their results and compare their holidays. To round off the activity, compare scores as a class to find out who had the best holiday.

**9** **LET'S TALK**   (V) *driving licence, memory card, phrase book, patron saint, capital, population* (P) *musician*

Read the instructions with your class. Have students choose five items from the list and divide them into groups of three or four. Distribute the dice, playing pieces and cards. Ask the groups to place the cards face down on the table and draw their attention to the start/finish square.

| HOME STUDY | Encourage students to expand the activities on the Home study page with their own ideas. Remind them that there are additional grammar activities in the Grammar and Vocabulary Booklet. |

**Homework suggestion**  As an additional optional homework assignment, you can invite students to choose one of the stories they told or topics they talked about in class and write it up. Offer to collect the stories in the following class for correction.

**Keys for Unit 4 – Part A**

**1.3** 1 Eric | 2 Susie | 3 Susie | 4 Eric | 5 Susie | 6 Susie

**2** 2 There were no budget airlines in the 80s. | 3 Air travel was only for the rich and famous. | 4 There was free in-flight food and drink 30 years ago. | 5 Aer Lingus and British Airways were the only airlines between London and Dublin.

**4** 1 visited | 2 moved | 3 wanted | 4 didn't plan | 5 closed | 6 talked | 7 didn't realize | 8 enjoyed | 9 arranged | 10 Did ... remember

**Language Box**   verb + ed | didn't + infinitive | did + infinitive

**5** 1 Did she stay with her sister for one night? | 2 Did they talk until late? | 3 Did they realize how late it was? | 4 Did she ask her neighbour to feed the cat?

**6** [t] helped, liked, watched | [d] answered, planned, stayed | [ɪd] decided, posted, waited

| Topics/Vocabulary | Pubs; everyday situations |
| --- | --- |
| Grammar | Simple past (irregular verbs) |
| Functions | Talking about the past; telling a story; everyday phrases |
| Home study | An Irish folk tale: Finn and Fingal |
| Photocopiable | Page 57 |
| Extra materials | 3 Tune In: A menu and/or pictures of the interior of a pub (optional) |

**Class opener** Invite students to tell or read out any stories or topics they may have written up as additional homework. Then write on the board, e.g. *Guinness, pint, brewery, music, games* and/or any other words connected to pubs which the students will already know. First ask your class what the connection between your words could be, then ask for more ideas connected to British and Irish pubs or any other type of pub, and add them to the board.

**1** ▭▭ **FOCUS** (V) *public, Romans, centuries, invaders, ale, customers, brewer, to pollute, community, groceries, sick, practical reasons, plenty*

Once students have read the instructions to **(1)**, draw their attention to the **Language Box**. Point out that the only difference between regular and irregular verbs concerns the verb forms and that negatives and questions work identically. Students then read the text and underline the irregular verbs individually. Check as a group.

Before or after **(2)**, you can add different activities focussing on irregular verbs. One option would be to ask your class which irregular verbs they know and collect them on the board. To make this more interactive, you can ask students to only say the infinitive while the rest of the class has to shout out the irregular form as quickly (and loudly) as possible. This could also be made into a team game.

Carry out **(2)** as presented in the coursebook. For **(3)**, divide the class into small groups. After a few minutes, invite students to share what they have found out with the rest of the class.

**2** ▭▭ **PRACTICE** Complete this activity as presented in the coursebook. To extend it, you could ask students, especially the faster ones, to add additional questions and answers based on the text.

**3** ▭▭ **TUNE IN** (V) *to get* (note the alternative usage), *to guess, coincidence, pint* (P) *coincidence, Yeats*

▭ 1 23  In pairs or individually, students complete the dialogue in **(1)**, then listen to check. To round off the activity, ask two students to read the conversation aloud. To begin **(2)**, ask the class to look at the instructions. After checking the phrase *last orders*, either have the whole group brainstorm and collect their ideas on the board or have them brainstorm in small groups first. Invite students to relate any personal experiences they have had with British and Irish pubs. In a less creative class you could offer different aspects on the board, e.g. the age of most customers, where to find pubs, what's on offer, music, or show a menu and/or pictures of the interior of a pub.

Differences between BE and AE often cause confusion of the words *chips* and *crisps*, both of which you can get in pubs. Point out that *crisps* is the BE term for the AE *potato chips*, whereas *chips* is the BE for the AE *French fries*. An easy way to remember *chips* is the typical *fish & chips* you can get in many pubs; explain that *crisps* are *knusprig*.

**4** ▭▭ **LET'S TALK** (V) *to circulate, to vote*

In **(1)**, students first put the story in the correct order. If students offer a different sequence of events than that suggested in the answer keys, invite them to explain how their story goes. Then proceed as presented in the coursebook. To give the slower teams more time, encourage the faster teams to add details to their stories. Focus on checking the use of the simple past, but do not correct too strictly. You can reward the winners with a small prize.

After students have read the instructions to **(2)**, give them a few minutes to make notes using keywords instead of full sentences. Ask the students to get up, find a partner and tell each other their stories. Time permitting, they should talk to at least three different people. Round off the activity by inviting the class to retell their favourite stories.

**Homework suggestion** As an additional optional homework assignment, you can invite students to write any story around the word *coincidence* similar to (1) in 4 Let's Talk as extra practice.

**5** OUT AND ABOUT
**(V)** *almost, owners, pub quiz, occasion, customary, rude*
For **(1)**, ask your class which Irish pubs they know of, in Ireland or anywhere in the world. Then ask them to read the text. Have students discuss the questions listed in **(2)** in small groups, and then compare their opinions as a class. Look at the **Culture Tip** together, then find out about your students' experiences with buying rounds and what they think about this approach. You can extend the discussion by asking what customs there are in their local pubs.

**6** OUT AND ABOUT

**(V)** *nuisance*
In **(1)**, students work in pairs to find matching responses. Point out that there are more responses than they need. You could expand this part by asking students to find suitable examples for the responses they have not used. Carry out **(2)** as presented in the coursebook. In pairs, students proceed with **(3)** as presented. To round off the activity, invite students to present their dialogues to the rest of the class.

**Optional photocopiable** This activity expands on the idea of 6 Out and about. Divide your class into pairs and distribute one set of cut-out sentences and responses to each pair. Once the teams have matched the sentences, you can give them a copy of the photocopiable so that they have the whole set to take home. Now ask them to get up, walk around the class and practise "throwing" phrases at each other and responding appropriately. After one exchange they should walk on and do the same at least once with every student in class. If you want to use the phrases to do some review of grammar or go into detail of the differences between e.g. *How are you?* and *How do you do?*, you can do this as a group before students walk around.

As an alternative to having the students walk around, you could give them a ball which the first student throws to another student. The catcher must respond to a random phrase that the thrower calls out. Then the catcher becomes the next thrower and so on.

**Homework suggestion** Ask students to think of any other frequent phrases they use in their native language. Encourage them to try and find the correct English counterpart and bring these phrases to the following class.

**HOME STUDY**
Encourage students to look up three more adjectives, ideally ones they themselves find useful, and write sentences as suggested in C Writing on the Home study page.

**Keys for Unit 4 – Part B**

**1.1** gave, came, went, was, drank, was, began, was, became, could, was, bought, took, did, didn't go, was, met, went

**1.2** 1 The Romans gave England its first pubs. I 2 Customers drank at the brewer's house. I 3 Alehouses became public houses, the centre of the community. I 4 Pubs are the place you go for a pint and 'craic'/fun.

**2** 1 When did the Romans give England its first pubs? They gave England its first pubs almost two thousand years ago. I 2 Why did they drink ale? Because it was not safe to drink the water. I 3 Where did people go to buy groceries? They didn't go to shops, they went to the public house. I

4 Did people only go to public houses for practical reasons? No, they also went there to meet friends.

**3.1** 1 What did he say? I 2 What did he mean? I 3 Did you go to I 4 Where did you learn English? I 5 What did you do there? I 6 Did you like it there? I 7 What did your sister do

**4.1** 1 B I 2 A I 3 E I 4 D I 5 C

**6.1** 1 Fine thanks, and you? I 2 It was great. I 3 What a shame. I 4 No problem. I 5 Oh, I'm sorry. I 6 Here you are, sir. I 7 What a nuisance! I 8 Happy birthday! I 9 Sure, go ahead.

# Part A Shopping

| | |
|---|---|
| **Topics/Vocabulary** | Princes Square; shopping; clothes; souvenirs |
| **Grammar** | *some/any*; *a lot of/lots of*; *much/many* |
| **Functions** | Describing clothes; talking with shop assistants |
| **Home study** | *some/any*, etc.; *much/many*; *a lot of/lots of*; adjectives; vocabulary work |
| **Photocopiable** | Page 58 |
| **Extra materials** | None |

**Class opener** Invite students to read some of the sentences they wrote for their Home study from Unit 4 Part B. Then introduce Unit 5 and the topic "shopping" by writing *The last thing I bought in a shop was …* on the board. Finish the sentence with an example of your own and add some more information, e.g. where you bought the item or why you bought it. As a class, students complete the sentence and add information.

**1** **FOCUS**
〔1〕26

(V) *bargain hunter, big spender, window-shopper, male/female, skirt, suits, underwear*
For **(1)**, ask the class to read the instructions and collect ideas about what the expressions mean. Then do a class poll to find out what kind of shoppers there are in the class. Invite students to say more about their shopping habits, e.g. the best bargain spots or areas for window-shopping. Before moving on to **(2)**, ask the class if they know any of the shop names pictured and what they sell. After **(2)**, direct the students to the **Language Box**. Give students time to read and fill in the gaps individually, then compare the answers as a group. To consolidate, play the recording again and ask students to take notes on the usage of *some* and *any* in the conversation. In a weaker class you could have the students read the transcript and mark the occurrences.

Students may have heard people ask *Would you like* <u>some</u> *more tea?* Tell them that in questions in which someone offers someone something, *some* is used rather than *any* and offer a few examples to illustrate the difference.

For **(3)**, students could discuss the questions in small groups. To play on the stereotypes a bit more, divide the class into men's and women's groups. After discussing in their separate gender groups, either mix the students to discuss in new groups, now with men and women, or discuss as a class.

**2** **PRACTICE**
(V) *department store, unusual, paperback, cuisine, extraordinary experience* (P) *unusual, cuisine*
Students could first read the complete text individually, then fill in the gaps with a partner. Then compare the answers as a class. To follow up, ask students why or why not Princes Square sounds like an inviting place to them and if they have ever been to any such shopping centres.

**3** **LET'S TALK**
In small groups or in pairs, students discuss the questions as presented in the coursebook.

**Homework suggestion** You could ask your students to compile a shopping guide for their area based on the information the groups collect in 3 Let's Talk. Alternatively, they could describe their favourite shop or shopping centre.

**4** **PRACTICE**
(V) *belt, bra, casual, dress, gloves, hat, necklace, scarf, smart, trainers, tie, tights* (P) *suit, tie*
Students fill in the table in **(1)** either in pairs or individually. Encourage them to use the vocabulary list in the coursebook to look up vocabulary they do not know. Have students do **(2)** in pairs to extend the table. Continue the pairwork in **(3)**. You can round off the activity by discussing dress codes at the workplace, at different events, etc.

As there are several clothing items that have different names in AE and BE, you might want to introduce the differences between them, e.g. pants, vest, sweater. Note that German students often mistake *trainers* (*fitness shoes/gym shoes/sneakers*) for *Trainingsanzug* (*track suit*).

**5** **LET'S TALK**
Carry out the activity as presented in the coursebook. As an alternative that offers the students an opportunity to move around, ask them to get up and stand in a circle. Give them a minute to look at their classmates, then tell them to turn around so that no one can see the others. Ask one student to say one thing about one of their fellow students, e.g. *I think Sabine is wearing red glasses.* The student named then has to say one thing about another student, etc. To keep the class

from always talking about the same people, you can also ask questions about particular students, e.g. *Henry, what is Sabine wearing?*

**6** LET'S TALK (V) and (P) *jewellery*

Students read the instructions and speech bubbles. Before dividing the class into small groups, you may want to give them a minute to take some notes and ask for vocabulary.

**7** FOCUS (V) *several*

Carry out (1) after giving students time to read through the gapped dialogue. Direct the students' attention to the **Language Box** and have them complete the rules. In (2), students discuss as described in the coursebook. After several minutes, you could ask the students to tell the class what they have found out about their partners.

**8** PRACTICE (V) and (P) *equipment*

Proceed as presented in the coursebook. Round off the activity by asking the class to report the most unusual findings to the group.

**9** LET'S TALK

Working individually, in (1) students match the sentences as described in the coursebook. Point out that the sentences do not make up one complete dialogue. To check, you could ask the class to read their matches. Once students have read the instructions to (2) and have formed pairs, tell them that they should write down and then read through the dialogue they create.

**Optional photocopiable**

(V) *kettle, towels, cosy, cushions, slippers, screwdriver, hammer, apron, oven gloves, fluffy* (P) *kettle, towels, cosy, cushion, apron*

This activity helps students use phrases for shopping and learn vocabulary for standard household items. Distribute one copy to each student. Give the students a few minutes to read the instructions and to read through the vocabulary list. Students then work with a partner. Encourage them to use the target language provided on the page.

As floors are numbered differently in BE and AE, you might want to introduce the differences here, e.g. *second floor* in BE can mean *third floor* in AE, etc.

HOME STUDY

Encourage students to expand the activities with their own ideas, e.g. C Adjectives. Remind them that word spiders might be a useful tool to group vocabulary into word fields.

**Keys for Unit 5 – Part A**

**1.2** Marks & Spencer sells underwear. I Debenhams sells cosmetics and clothes. I Waterstone's sells books. I Next sells clothes and shoes.

**Language Box** some I any

**2** 1 a I 2 some I 3 some I 4 some I 5 any I 6 any I 7 a I 8 some I 9 a I 10 a I 11 some I 12 an

**4.1 Clothes:** blouse, bra, dress, pullover, shirt, skirt, socks, suit, tights, trousers, underwear I **Accessories:** belt, earrings, gloves, handbag, hat, necklace, scarf, tie I

**Footwear:** boots, slippers, trainers I **Style:** casual, smart, sporty

**7.1** 1 lots of I 2 many I 3 much I 4 many I 5 much I 6 lots of I 7 lots of I 8 lots of I 9 much I 10 many

**Language Box** a lot of / lots of I many/much

**9.1** 1 Can I help you? (A) I 2 I'm just looking, thanks. (S) I 3 How would you like to pay? (A) I 4 I'm looking for a size 12. (S) I 5 Have you got anything in black? (S) I 6 I'd like to look at some earrings. (S) I 7 Would you like to try it on? (A)

| Topics/Vocabulary | The Edinburgh Festival; Scotland; Burns Night; the Scottish Country Dancers of Hamburg |
| --- | --- |
| Grammar | Present perfect |
| Functions | Talking about experiences in the past |
| Home study | Cape Breton's Celtic Colours International Festival |
| Photocopiable | Page 59 |
| Extra materials | Class opener: A4 paper; 2 Practice: Blank cards (optional) |

**Class opener**  To revise the vocabulary for clothing and accessories from Part A, hand out one piece of A4 paper to each person. Have students fold it into thirds horizontally. On the first third, the first person draws a head, adding appropriate pieces of clothing, accessories, etc. After passing the pieces of paper clockwise, the next person draws from the neck to the waist on the second third. The paper is passed again and the legs and feet are drawn by the next person on the lowest third. Pass them again. The fourth student unfolds the paper and describes the "person" on it.

To transition to the topic of "festivals" presented in Part B, ask the students *At which festivals do people wear special clothing or costumes?* To extend the activity, you could ask students to describe the clothing the best they can with the vocabulary they already know.

**1**  FOCUS  (V) *street performer, foreign, piper, tattoo, to look forward to + ing* (P) *Edinburgh*
Give students time to expand on **(1)** and encourage them to say more about any festivals they know, e.g. what kind of festivals they are, when and where they take place, etc. Avoid correcting the simple past and present perfect for the time being. Note the festivals mentioned: you could use them again at the end of **(2)**.

Refer the group to the **Language Box** and ask them to find examples for the two tenses in 1 Focus before filling in the gaps. Point out that when people talk about an experience they have had in their lives, they use the present perfect to state the general experience without a connection to a specific time and then often switch to the simple past to provide additional details regarding what they did or saw. Once the difference is clear, tell the students to read the instructions for **(2)**.

Together, refer to the festivals mentioned by the students in **(1)**, then ask *Have you been to any of these festivals?* and if yes, follow up with *What did you do/see there?* At this point, pay increased attention to the correct usage of the tenses. Keep the discussion short, as students will have to discuss similar questions in pairs in 3 Tune In.

For many German learners, the difference between the simple past and present perfect is one of the most problematic English grammar topics. Be prepared to supply students with additional examples to explain the different usages of the two tenses, e.g. *I have been to Asia twice. I went to Thailand in ... and did some trekking in Nepal ... years ago.*

**2**  PRACTICE  (V) and (P) *juggler*
Carry out as presented in the coursebook and encourage the class to make more examples.

To build knowledge of irregular verbs and their past participles (also known as the "third form" to many German students) by means of a quick game, distribute about 10 blank cards to each student and ask them to write the infinitive of an irregular verb on one side of a card and the two irregular past forms (simple past and the past participle) on the back. They then swap their stacks with other students and find a partner. After shuffling the cards, they place the stack in front of them with the infinitive side up. Student A takes the first card and says the past forms. Then it's Student B's turn. A right answer gets a point; a wrong answer loses a point. For a weaker class, you could refer students to the list of irregular verbs on p. 60 in the Grammar and Vocabulary Booklet to create their cards but encourage them to keep it closed during the game.

**3**  TUNE IN  (V) *incredible*
1 28  Carry out **(1)** as presented. For **(2)**, students discuss the questions in pairs. Listen in to check for the correct usage of the simple past and present perfect. You could round off the activity by asking the

class if they have learned about any festivals they would like to attend and why they would want to attend them.

**4** **LET'S TALK** Once students have read the instructions and sample dialogue, they first complete the questions. Then ask them to mingle and encourage them to talk to as many of their classmates as possible. After a few minutes, students can report their findings to the group.

**5** **LET'S TALK** After the class has read the instructions to **(1)**, you may want to check the structure by asking a few students to ask an actual question and writing at least one of them on the board, e.g. *Who has eaten fish & chips?* Explain that if they cannot find any commonalities in their group, the answer could be *There isn't any food we have all eaten*. Proceed to **(2)** as presented in the coursebook.

 **Optional photocopiable** Divide the class into two groups. Give each group the upper or lower half of the photocopiable, and then ask them to find a partner from the other group. The pairs then exchange information to fill in the gaps on their respective pages. Encourage students not to look at each other's copies.

 As it may sound and look confusing, pre-teach the structure *have had* for possession prior to beginning the photocopiable activity.

**6** **SOUND CHECK** Proceed with **(1)** and **(2)** as presented in the coursebook. For **(3)**, collect your students' ideas on the board or ask them to write them on the board themselves. Browse the Internet prior to class to find additional examples.
**1 29**
**1 30**

**7** **OUT AND ABOUT** (V) *bagpipe, wedding, kilt, tartan, poetry, haggis, oats, address, lassies*
Have students do **(1)** individually. After checking the answers with the class and before turning to **(2)**, look at the **Culture Tips**. Ask the class if they know any other such tips for dealing with people from Scotland and if there are any such things to keep in mind about the people in the area they are from (e.g. never mix up Bavarians and Austrians). Keep it short. In **(2)**, pairs discuss the questions as presented and after a few minutes report their findings to the group.

**8** **ENGLISH NEAR ME** After playing the audio and comparing the answers with the class, ask your class if they know of similar classes or clubs in their area (be it Scottish dancing or square dance) and what they think about these types of clubs.
**1 31**

**HOME STUDY** Draw your students' attention to the puzzle on the Home study page and the written homework in C Writing. Ask them to make their own puzzles and bring them to the next class, ideally with copies for all students.

## Keys for Unit 5 – Part B

**Language Box** present perfect I simple past

**2** 2 Have you ever heard a piper? Yes, I have. I heard a Scottish one in August. I 3 Have your neighbours ever had a party? Yes, they have. They had a noisy one last weekend. I 4 Has your cat ever caught a mouse? Yes, it has. It caught a little one last night. I 5 Have you ever forgotten a birthday? Yes, I have. I forgot an important one last month.

**3.1** 1 Yes, she has. I 2 Yes, she has. I 3 Yes, she has. I 4 No, she hasn't. I 5 No, she hasn't.

**6.1** cheap I ship I cash I shoe I shop I which

**6.2** She chatted to Sasha and Charlie in front of the fish and chip shop. I She watched the washing machine wash her watch.

**7.1** Line 11 'here' should be 'hear' I Line 28 'live' should be 'life' I Line 35 'plate' should be 'dish' I Line 40 'eat' should be 'meal' I Line 43 'mans' should be 'men' I Line 47 'dead' should be 'death'

**8** 1 T I 2 F I 3 T I 4 F I 5 T I 6 F

# WORK

## Part A **Looking back**

| | |
|---|---|
| **Topics/Vocabulary** | Wales; working life |
| **Grammar** | Simple past and *used to* |
| **Functions** | Talking about the way things used to be; talking about work |
| **Home study** | (*never*) *used to*; simple past; vocabulary work |
| **Photocopiable** | Page 60 |
| **Extra materials** | **3 Let's Talk:** Same-sized pieces of paper for each student |

**Class opener** Begin by asking students to swap the puzzles they made for the Home study in Unit 5 Part B and to complete their partner's puzzle. Put the following names on the board: Anthony Hopkins (actor), Catherine Zeta-Jones (actress), Charlotte Church (singer), Tom Jones (singer). Before they open their coursebooks, ask students what the names have in common. These people are all Welsh. Ask if anyone has been to Wales.

**1**  **FOCUS** | 2 02 | (V) *Celtic, status, bilingual, education* (P) *bilingual*

Carry out **(1)** as a class. Then proceed to **(2)**. Give the students a minute to complete the quiz, and then listen to check the answers. You could do a class poll to see how many people guessed correctly. Now direct students' attention to the **Language Box**. You could point out that *used to* is used in a similar way as the German word *früher* for things that were true in the past but which are no longer true. To ensure students' understanding, you could divide the class into pairs and have them turn to the audio transcript on p.104. Using the facts provided in the transcript, ask each pair to form one positive sentence, one negative sentence, and one question that all use a form of *used to*. Many answers are possible.

> Make sure that students read the yellow post-it at the bottom of the page. Emphasize that *in former times* is rarely, if ever, used by English speakers and that we usually express *früher* by using the simple past.

**2**  **PRACTICE** | 2 03 | (V) *shopkeeper, character, wig, gate, turkey, to be able to afford, country people* (P) *wig*

Carry out **(1)** as presented in the coursebook. You could ask students to write out both the full question and answer, underlining both *used to* forms. In **(2)**, some students may be confused by Question 3, as it uses the formation of *used to* usually found in a positive statement. If this point comes up, explain that that question refers to "you" and not the past action of Mr Baker. Do **(3)** as either a class discussion or in small groups; encourage each student to contribute.

**3** **LET'S TALK** Carry out **(1)** and **(2)** as presented in the coursebook.

> Use your own paper here, as otherwise students might know who the paper belongs to prior to carrying out the activity.

 **Optional photocopiable**
(V) *to be bald, car park/parking lot, playground*
Divide the class into pairs, then hand out a copy of the photocopiable to each student. Ask them to take it in turns to read out what they understand from the pictures based on the example given. Their partner then says if he or she feels the answer is right or not and continues.

**4** **TUNE IN** | 2 04 | (V) *coal mining, uncertain, pit, unemployed, countryside, to get a promotion, shift manager, to borrow* (P) *uncertain*

Prior to reading the instructions, read out three or four random years and then have students come up and write their answers on the board. Write a few additional years on the board and check pronunciation with a few volunteers. Then proceed as in the coursebook.

> *Borrow* (*to borrow s.th. from s.o.*) and *lend* (*to lend s.th. to s.o.*) are often confusing. Demonstrate the difference: e.g. *Christian, could I borrow your pen? Thanks. Christian lent his pen to me.*

**5** **LET'S TALK** (V) *like* (note the alternative usage)
For **(1)**, students should write out the complete questions to help solidify their knowledge. You might want to point out the difference between Questions 1 and 4.

Before moving to **(2)**, you could give students a few minutes to make some notes and write down key vocabulary words they will need. Have students ask their partner questions to show interest and get more information. For example: *The biggest change in my life was when we moved to Berlin. – When was that? – It was in 1993. – What changed for you? – We both had new jobs. We lived in a big city.* Students could then talk to a second person in the class.

**6** `PRACTICE` (V) *flexitime, salary, suit, wages* (P) *suit*

Before starting the activity, write the headings in the book on the board and elicit as many work-related words from the students as possible. Then have the students do **(1)** and check as a class, adding the words to the board. Students could work in pairs to complete **(2)**. After working individually for **(3)**, students could read one of their sentences to the class. To extend **(3)**, you could ask the rest of the class to try to think of a question based on the sentence the student reads. Building on the example answer in the text, you could write the following questions on the board: *What colour was your uniform? Where was the café?*

**7** `LET'S TALK` (V) *to care about, security*

Give students time to read through the survey in **(1)** and write in the ratings for themselves. Then divide the class into groups of three or four. The students should first compare results. Then they can turn to **(2)**, adding two additional points and repeating the process of rating and comparing. With the full class, you could then ask each group if everyone had the same opinion about the most/least important points and to name them, or take a class poll.

**8** `LET'S TALK` Encourage students to use the new structure from the lesson (*used to*) during the activity. Ask students to find a new partner and proceed as presented in the coursebook.

As you close the lesson, draw attention to the **Culture Tip** at the top of the page. Tell the students that as they leave the room they should exchange the phrases with one of their classmates.

**HOME STUDY** Encourage students to do the activities in the Home study. You can listen to their stories about D Jane's life at the beginning of the next lesson to check their answers.

**Keys for Unit 6 – Part A**

**1.2** T | T | F

**2.1** She used to live in a small village.

**2.2** 1 The shopkeepers used to speak Welsh. |
2 She used to wear a wig because she didn't have much hair. She weighed potatoes with her hands. If you wanted a cake, she used to put it in the bag with the potatoes using the same dirty hands. |
3 Mr Baker used to cook the turkeys at Christmas because he had a big oven. |
4 She used to speak Welsh at home.

**4** 2 1989 pit closed; lost his job | 1990 unemployed; went on a retraining course |

1992 stopped training; looked for a job | 1993 started bus driving; enjoyed driving around the Welsh countryside | 1997 got promotion; became shift manager | 2007 mobile library job; felt happier than when he was a miner

**5.1** 1 was | 2 did | 3 did | 4 was | 5 did | 6 did

**6.1** **Dress:** overalls, suit, uniform | **Pay:** bonus, salary, wages | **Workplace:** factory, office, shop | **Working hours:** flexitime, 9–5, shifts

**6.2** 1 overalls | 2 bonus | 3 shifts | 4 suit | 5 flexitime

| Topics/Vocabulary | In the office; team-building and fitness in an office |
| --- | --- |
| **Grammar** | Simple past and past progressive |
| **Functions** | Office communication; situating past events |
| **Home study** | The English and the Welsh |
| **Photocopiable** | Page 61 |
| **Extra materials** | None |

**Class opener**  Students who did D Jane's life from the Home study could read their stories aloud, as it might be interesting for the class to hear the different variations. After that, transition to the new topic: to get a feeling of their experience and confidence with English phone calls, ask students if they have any experience using English on the telephone either at work or in their free time. You could ask more questions to elicit when the call took place and why. Or the person who most recently spoke with someone in English on the phone could describe the call and his or her handling of it.

**1  FOCUS**  2 05

(V) *to put s.o. through, purse, pickpocket* (P) *busy, brochure, castle*

Ask the class the questions in **(1)**. Prior to **(2)**, give students time to read the six phrases, then play the recording twice if necessary. It might be helpful to write the six phrases on the board in a list and then add the equivalent as you check the activity with the class.

Transition to the **Language Box**, illustrating the difference between simple past and past progressive on the board. Be prepared to write additional examples, e.g. *When I was coming to class today, I saw a big dog.* You could then ask a few students what happened or what they saw as they were coming to class and add their answers to the board. Use two different colours to mark the respective verb forms on the board. Ask the students to fill in the two gaps in the Language Box. After checking, direct the students to do **(3)** individually or in pairs. After checking **(3)**, proceed with **(4)** as presented in the coursebook. If **(4)** is carried out in small groups, you could then ask each group for the most interesting or surprising answer.

> To help students remember which tense is which, you could tell them that the tense with the longer name, past progressive, is used for the longer action: *I was looking for my purse when my daughter came home.*

**2  PRACTICE**

(V) *to spill s.th., to break down*

In pairs or individually, have students complete **(1)** as presented in the coursebook. Have students try to spot both conjunctions (*while/when*) that are commonly used with the past progressive. Before having the students begin **(2)** in pairs, provide an example on the board: *I was listening to the teacher when my mobile rang. I answered the phone while I was running out of the room.* Give students time to talk to their partners, then ask each student to tell the class one thing their partner said.

**3  PRACTICE**

(V) *bin, filing cabinet*

Start by asking students to close their books and tell you what they expect to find in an office. Write their suggestions on the board and then do **(1)** as presented in the coursebook. Before pairing off the students for **(2)**, explain that they are going to form sentences describing what was taking place at the point of time when Ann left. You could illustrate this on the board using the example given, drawing a dot for Ann's point of leaving at 5 pm and a long line for what Diane was doing. In a weaker class, you could ask them to write the sentences instead of just saying them.

**Optional photocopiable**  Ask students to stand or sit in a circle and give each a card. Explain that this activity is about actions in the past which were in progress "when the boss walked in". Tell them that they have to mime the action on the card for the others to guess. Give them time to plan their actions. You could read out or mime the following example to get them started:
Group: *What were you doing when the boss walked in?*
Student: (mimes the action, e.g. drinking from a bottle of water)
Group: *You were drinking something, weren't you? / Drinking? / Were you drinking something?*
Student: (nods and takes another swig from the bottle)

Repeat around the circle, or proceed with the group member who guessed the answer correctly. Encourage students to help each other with any vocabulary.

**4** **LET'S TALK** Proceed as directed in the coursebook. Walk around the class and listen to their dialogues. Invite students to act out their dialogues in front of the rest of the class. For an extra challenge in a stronger class, have the students sit back to back so they can't read each other's lips. Time permitting, have them work out an additional dialogue.

**5** **LET'S TALK** Have the students complete the table and check the answers with the class. Ensure that students have new partners for the second part of the activity. To check question structures, ask the students how they would form some of the questions, e.g. *When did you last send an email? / When was the last time you sent an email?* Point out that many verbs will require irregular forms in the answers.

**6** **OUT AND ABOUT** (V) *to depend on s.o. or s.th., design, emphasis, woodland, to monitor, setting* (P) *emphasis*
Begin by asking your students if they have ever done any team-building seminars or similar activities at work. You could include other social events which help team building, such as Christmas or summer events. Students do **(1)** individually as presented in the coursebook. Encourage students to find a new partner before starting **(2)**. After a few minutes, have the pairs report their opinions on **(2)** to the class. You could also tally the responses to see which team-building activities are the most popular. Can your class agree on one activity? Where could they do that activity?

**7** **OUT AND ABOUT** **2 06** (V) *physically, to advise s.o. to do s.th., to improve, to reduce, opposite, cheap rates, excuse, to invest in* (P) *reducing, opposite*
Give students time to read the sentences in **(1)**, then play the recording. After checking the answers, do **(2)** as presented in the coursebook. As an extension, ask the students to brainstorm any small step they or their workplace could take to create a less stressful work setting.

**HOME STUDY** Encourage students to read the text for homework. Many may remember the film. Ask students to bring their sentences from C Writing to the next lesson. You could begin the next lesson by having the students read out what they wrote and having the others guess the film.

## Keys for Unit 6 – Part B

**1.2** 1 I'll get back to you. | 2 Could you hold the line, please? | 3 How can I help you? | 4 ... talk to you in a bit. | 5 Could you put me through to ..., please? | 6 I'm ringing about ...

**1.3** **simple past:** tried, weren't, did (you) call, was, lost, stole, emailed |
**past progressive:** was showing, wasn't looking, wasn't working

**Language Box** past progressive | simple past

**2.1** 1 She phoned him while he was walking around the castle. | 2 A pickpocket took her purse while she was having tea. | 3 We were driving to Wales when our car broke down. | 4 I spilt coffee on the keyboard while I was talking to a colleague. | 5 He was sitting in a meeting when his mobile rang.

**3.1** 1 photocopier | 2 monitor | 3 filing cabinet | 4 lamp | 5 mouse | 6 keyboard | 7 desk | 8 coffee machine | 9 bin | 10 printer

**5** **a call:** to make, to get, to answer, to take |
**a coffee:** to make, to get, to have |
**a break:** to get, to take, to have |
**a meeting:** to have

**6.1** People do such courses to learn to work together as a team.

**7.1** 1 T | 2 DK | 3 F | 4 T | 5 F | 6 DK

| Topics/Vocabulary | Preparing for a holiday; entering Canada; rules and signs; coping with stress |
| --- | --- |
| Grammar | Modal auxiliaries |
| Functions | Giving advice |
| Home study | Modal auxiliaries; vocabulary work |
| Photocopiable | Page 62 |
| Extra materials | None |

**Class opener**  To lead up to the topic of holidays, ask students to brainstorm and write down three things that would be part of a dream holiday for them. As this is supposed to be a quick warm-up, tell the class that they will only have a minute to do this. After students compare with their neighbours, collect the ideas as a class, then turn to 1 Focus.

**1  FOCUS**  2 08  **(V)** *in theory, ought to, relatives, passport, to renew* **(P)** *ought to*

Ask your students for their ideas in response to the question posed in **(1)** and collect the answers in a word spider on the board. Leave the answers on the board so you can use them later. Before playing the recording in **(2)**, ask students to read all statements and check for unknown vocabulary. When reviewing the answers, ask students to read out the answers using Jake's and Ellen's names, i.e. *Jake has to ....* or *Ellen has to ....* Then turn to the **Language Box**. After reading the information presented, ask your students to use the modal auxiliaries there to make sentences with the ideas you collected on the board in **(1)**. If any students make the mistake described on the post-it note, point out the use of *needn't* and *mustn't* immediately. If not, look at it with your class before turning to the next activity.

Students often have problems with using *had to* as the past tense of *must* and *wasn't/weren't allowed to* for *mustn't*. For further practice, divide your class into pairs and ask students to think about some examples of things they had to do or weren't allowed to do in their past holidays. Each team writes down at least two sentences for each of the two structures. Round off by asking students to read out their sentences.

**2  PRACTICE**  **(V)** *amazing, forms, visa*

Carry out as presented in the coursebook in pairs or ask students to first underline the answers individually and then discuss with a partner. Compare as a class.

**3  PRACTICE**  **(V)** *advice, temporary, purpose, to consider, valid, duration, port of entry, (a) few, remain, to support yourself, dependants* **(P)** *purpose*

Students read the text and all rules individually. After checking for unknown vocabulary, divide your class into pairs. Ask them to discuss the rules and encourage them to use the phrases below the rules while doing so. Give students a few minutes and ask them to only turn to p. 94 when you tell them. Round off by asking which of the rules the students found surprising; see if any of them has had any experience with either Canadian or any other customs and immigration rules.

**Optional photocopiable**

**(V)** *aisle, departure, charge, cabin crew, seatbelt, to fasten*

For this activity you need one copy of the photocopiable for each student and one set of cut-out sentences per group of three or four students. First hand out one copy of the photocopiable to each student and ask them to fill in the modal verbs given. After checking the answers in class, divide the students into groups and ask them to put the completed photocopiables away. Give each group a set of the cut-out, incomplete sentences and ask them to place them face down on the table. In turn, each student takes a sentence and reads the incomplete sentence aloud for the others. The first player who says the missing modal verb is given the sentence.

**4  LET'S TALK**  **(V)** *sign, gopher, permit;* for describing the signs: *to watch out for (s.th.), moose/elk, disabled, truck/lorry, buffalo*

Proceed with **(1)** as presented in the coursebook and explain difficult vocabulary if necessary. Encourage students to use the modal auxiliaries presented in the Language Box in 1 Focus to talk about the signs in this step as well as in **(2)**. Discuss the students' ideas as a class.

**Homework suggestion** You can invite your students to find unusual signs (in any language) on the Internet. Ask them to bring a printout of the signs along to the following class and to be prepared to explain what you have to do, aren't allowed to do, etc. when you see the signs.

**5** **LET'S TALK** (V) *to cope (with), rush hour, public transport, instead, weeknight, hire*
Students first note down three things as described in the coursebook. Before dividing the class into groups, direct the students to look at the pieces of advice presented in the speech bubbles to give the class an idea of what the responses could be like. After students have worked with their groups for a few minutes, round off by asking the class for the best advice they were given to fight stress.

**6** **TUNE IN** (V) *to feel/get stressed out, flight attendant, deadlines, to identify (with)*
**2 09** Do **(1)** as presented in the coursebook. Only play the recording once, as students will listen again in the next step. After a quick check, ask your students to read **(2)** and to be prepared to take notes while listening to the recording the second time. After the pairs have discussed their answers, compare as a class. Have students find new partners before starting **(3)** and then carry out the instructions provided. Round off by asking your class to report back any interesting points.

**7** **SOUND CHECK** (V) *in order to*
**2 10** For **(1)**, ask your students to first listen to the recording, then mark the correct stress patterns; ask students to read out the words to check. Before turning to **(2)**, you can invite your students to expand the list with up to five more three-syllable words. If they need help, either ask them to find words within this part of the unit (e.g. *probably, consider*) or refer them to the word list. Students then do **(2)** either individually or in pairs. Round off the activity by inviting the class to read out their texts.

As the writing task is the last activity in this part, you could ask students to write the text as homework, especially if you are running short of time.

**HOME STUDY** Encourage students to expand D Vocabulary by thinking of alternative answers.

### Keys for Unit 7 – Part A

**1.2** 1 Ellen I 2 Jake I 3 Jake I 4 Jake I 5 Jake I 6 Ellen I 7 Ellen

**2** 1 shouldn't I 2 ought to I 3 should I 4 don't have to I 5 had to I 6 have to I 7 ought to I 8 don't have to

**3** 1 false I 2 true I 3 true I 4 false I 5 true I 6 false

**4** 1 You must/have to stop. I 2 You should/must/have to leave after eight hours.; You aren't allowed to have a fire.; You aren't allowed to camp overnight.; You should watch out for gopher holes. I 3 You should watch out for moose/elk for the next five kilometres. I 4 Only disabled people or drivers with disabled people in the car are allowed to park here. You have to have a permit to park here. I 5 You aren't allowed to turn right on red. I 6 You have to go in one direction. I 7 You should watch out for large trucks. I 8 You should watch out for buffalo.

**6.2** Jeff takes a hot bath, cooks something, does things he likes and talks to a friend. I Gloria does yoga, has a glass of wine and listens to jazz. I Janet runs three miles a day and she doesn't eat meat, watch the news or read the newspapers.

**7.1** oOo = relaxing, consider, important I Ooo = exercise, healthily, alcohol, vegetable

# Part B Talking about the future

| | |
|---|---|
| **Topics/Vocabulary** | Holiday in space; forever young; Indian hobbyists; a Blackfoot in Potsdam |
| **Grammar** | Future with *will* |
| **Functions** | Making predictions; completing a questionnaire |
| **Home study** | The worliday: combining work and holidays |
| **Photocopiable** | Page 63 |
| **Extra materials** | **3 Let's Talk:** A3 paper (optional) |

**Class opener** If you assigned the Homework suggestion in Part A following 4 Let's Talk, you could invite students to present their signs. This could either be done as a quiz or as a mini-presentation. If you asked students to write the texts in 7 Sound Check Step (2) for homework, you could invite students to read out their texts about healthy living.

**1** FOCUS
2 11
(V) *founded, customers, to receive, to set off, breathtaking, street performer, foundation, charity, poverty, to contain* (P) *to receive, breathtaking*

In small groups, students discuss **(1)**. After reporting back to the class, students individually do **(2)** as presented in the coursebook. If necessary, clarify unknown vocabulary before playing the recordings. Check as a class, then go over the **Language Box** together.

The future with *will* often causes two kinds of problems for German learners. Firstly, as the German *Ich will* looks like *I will* many students use *will* instead of *want* (e.g. ~~I will a raise.~~ instead of *I want a raise.*). Secondly, the shortened form *won't* for *will not* is not as easily recognizable as the negative form of, e.g. *don't* for *do not*. Draw your students' attention to these two problems and invite them to find some examples of their own that illustrate the differences and the correct usages.

Many students confuse *to find* with *to found* because of the irregular past tense form of *find*. Point out the difference between the two verbs by writing *to find → found* and *to found → founded* on the board.

**2** PRACTICE
Once students have read the task instructions, draw their attention to the post-it note. Point out the difference between the use of *will* for predicting things and the present progressive for talking about arrangements. To refresh their memories about this kind of use of the present progressive, you can refer students to the grammar section of Unit 3. Once you have clarified the difference between the two future forms, students choose the correct verb form individually before comparing answers as a class.

**3** LET'S TALK
(V) *inventions*

Divide your class into pairs, then have the pairs carry out the activity as presented in the coursebook. Encourage the students to think of additional aspects and to take notes about their ideas and answers. Give students sufficient time to talk before comparing answers and additional ideas as a class. Alternatively, you could distribute one sheet of A3 paper to each pair and ask them to make a poster that illustrates their answers and ideas. Collect the posters and put them on the board or on different walls for the class to look at. Invite students to have a look at the different posters and to discuss them with their partners or as a class.

**4** LET'S TALK
(V) *add, subtract, occasional, moderate*

Read **(1)** with your class and point out that the questionnaire should not be taken too seriously. Before turning to **(2)**, find out who in your class will live the longest. For **(2)**, you can divide the class either into random groups or form groups of students from different parts on the lifespan scale. Encourage students to write down the ideas they brainstorm in their groups. After a few minutes, discuss the groups' ideas as a class.

**Optional photocopiable**
**(V)** *environment, to protect*
This activity aims to revise the use of will for predictions. Hand out a copy of the photocopiable to each student. Students first complete the mind maps with different topics, then interview their partners for their predictions. (It might be helpful for students to have a few minutes to formulate the questions before pairing off.) You could ask the students to take notes so that they can share some predictions with the class. Try to keep things positive as best you can.

**5**

**(V)** *hobbyists, powwow, teepee, beads, passionate, novels, characters, themes, published*
While the class reads the instructions to **(1)**, write *North American Indian* on the left side of the board and *hobbyists* on the right, then collect your students' ideas on the board. Invite students who have personal experience as Indian hobbyists to say something about their hobby. After reading the text, clarify vocabulary if necessary and then compare the content with the ideas on the board as a class. Divide the class into small groups for **(2)**. After students have discussed the questions for several minutes, ask them to report back to the class.

**6** ENGLISH NEAR ME
2 12

**(V)** *indigenous tribes, to board (with), tribal chief, counsellor, government, elected, economic growth, role model, to purify, dome-shaped, diameter, physically, spiritually, to aim to, to assume*
Give students time to read the instructions and the questions, then play the recording and repeat if necessary. As an alternative for a weaker group, you could play the recording before students read the questions and repeat after they have read them. Ask the class if they know any other Native American Indians in their area and invite students to talk about their experiences. To round off the lesson, read the **Culture Tip**. You can extend this idea by talking about whether the situation is similar e.g. for Bavarians and Austrians, Austrians and Swiss, and people from Berlin and Hamburg.

HOME STUDY

Encourage students to do the writing task on the Home study page. As an alternative topic you can suggest students write about their own experience with "worlidays". Remind your students to look at the Lerntipp on p. 59 and encourage them to try out the reading strategy suggested there.

**Keys for Unit 7 – Part B**

**1.2** 1 will | 2 won't | 3 will | 4 won't | 5 will | 6 will

**2** 1 will find | 2 will enjoy | 3 are meeting | 4 am working | 5 will never go | 6 will have

**6** 1 When he was a child he liked fishing, horseback riding, hiking and bicycle riding. | 2 He grew up on the Peigan Reserve in southern Alberta. | 3 He went to high school in Calgary. | 4 Job creation, education and economic growth were important to his father when he was a tribal chief. | 5 He moved in 1997 to experience living in another country. | 6 Different tribes perform dances in a three-day event. | 7 The sweat lodge purifies the body and the spirit through steam. | 8 The Blackfoot people live in the modern world. They live in houses, not teepees.

# UNIT 8 PROS AND CONS

## Part A  The media

| | |
|---|---|
| **Topics/Vocabulary** | Youth and media; statistics; TV shows; TV schedules |
| **Grammar** | Comparison of adjectives; *more/most, less/least, few/fewer/fewest*; prepositions of time; ordinal numbers; the date |
| **Functions** | Making comparisons; talking about statistics; giving dates |
| **Home study** | American/British English; *more/most, less/least*; comparison(s); vocabulary work |
| **Photocopiable** | Page 64 |
| **Extra materials** | **9 Let's Talk:** A3 pieces of paper for each small group |

**Class opener**  Begin by asking students to put any form of electronic media they have with them on the desk and to tell you what other forms they own. Ask students for their ideas about such media. You could ask questions such as *What are the advantages and disadvantages of such media? What age do you think children should have their first mobile phone? Is there an age limit for such technology?*

**1 ▮▮▮▮ FOCUS**
**2 14**

(V) *average, to spend (time), every waking hour, pockets, buddies, survey, to get along with*
(P) *average, unhappier*
Move on to **(1)** and carry out as presented in the coursebook. You could draw a table on the board to record who spends how much time using electronic media, e.g. 30 minutes per day, 1–2 hours per day, or whatever categories seem appropriate for your class. Keep the table on the board to refer to later. Then ask the students to read the text and fill in the gaps for **(2)**. Play the recording to allow students to check their answers. Go through the **Language Box** with the class and point out that short (one-syllable) adjectives take *-er* and *-est*, adjectives ending in *-y* become *-ier* and adjectives with two or more syllables take *more* or *most*. Point out the exceptions of *good* and *bad*. Students could identify the different forms in the text from **(2)**. You could then return to the table from **(1)** and ask students to form sentences using *less, more*, and *the most* about their classmates' electronic media habits.

Proceed with **(3)** as presented in the coursebook, either as a class discussion or in groups which report back.

Students often confuse the German *spenden* with *to spend*. Introduce the English verb *to donate* as the translation for the German *spenden*.

Be on the lookout for students who try to use *as* instead of *than* to form the comparative due to the German use of *als*.

**2 ▮▮▮▮ PRACTICE**

(V) *anti-social*
Carry out the activity as presented in the coursebook. Write the table on the board and ask for volunteers to come up and complete the table. Then working in pairs, students create a "quiz" for another pair by collecting six additional adjectives (without the comparative and superlative forms) on a piece of paper. They then swap with another pair, who must add the comparative and superlative forms.

**3 ▮▮▮▮ LET'S TALK**

Proceed as presented in the coursebook. Round off this activity with a class discussion on the topics in the sentences, making sure the discussion stays positive.

**4 ▮▮▮▮ FOCUS**

(P) *photography*
First draw the students' attention to the **Language Box** and read through the examples together. To help consolidate their knowledge, have one student form a sentence using *more ... than*, the next student has to turn this sentence into a superlative with *most*. The next student should form a different sentence with *less ... than*, the next uses this sentence in the superlative with *least*. The fifth person makes a sentence using *few*, etc., going around the room so that everyone has at least one turn.
Move on to **(1)** as presented in the coursebook as a class. Collect ideas for **(2)** on the board as a class in the form of a vertical list with suggestions for *the most* at the top and *the least* at the bottom according to students' answers.

Point out that in the short forms of million and billion, a dot is used in English and not a comma, and that *m* is the abbreviation for *million* and not *mio*. You could also mention that *Milliarde* is *billion* in English.

**5** PRACTICE (V) *recreational, increase*
Proceed as in the coursebook, perhaps in pairs, and check answers together.

**6** LET'S TALK Proceed with both **(1)** and **(2)** as described in the coursebook. If students need help finding additional topics for **(1)**, you could refer them to 4 Focus for some ideas.

**7** FOCUS (V) *traffic, freeway, to record, judge, divorced, to run, chef* (P) *divorced*
**2 15** Proceed with **(1)** as described in the coursebook. In a weaker class, have the students read **(2)** before listening. Check answers to **(2)** as a class and have students name the shows they never miss. Transition to the **Language Box**. Write *at, in* and *on* on the board and ask the students to give additional examples, e.g. *on Monday, at 6 am, in November*. Go through the ordinal numbers in the box and point out the differences between British and American English when saying dates.

**8** PRACTICE Students can complete **(1)** individually as directed in the coursebook. Collect ideas for the first question in **(2)** together on the board and discuss as a class. Then ask students to write down three dates which are important to them and see if a partner can guess what happened or happens on those dates. Encourage students to ask each other questions to find out more about the dates mentioned and to report back any interesting findings to the class.

**9** LET'S TALK Ask the class the questions in **(1)** and then divide your students into small groups before proceeding with **(2)**. Ideas could be written on the board or each group could put their ideas on an A3 piece of paper which could be put up. At the end, you could vote for the best and worst TV show and discuss as a class why you came to that conclusion.

**Optional photocopiable**
(V) *golf shots, to occur, file, pocket, traffic jam, lane, damage, pile* (P) *to occur*
The photocopiable gives students a chance to see comparables and superlatives in context. Hand out a copy of the photocopiable to each student. Students work alone or in pairs to match the sentence halves. The final questions can first be discussed by pairs or small groups and then opened to the class. The class could vote on the truest, the best, or the funniest suggestion(s).

HOME STUDY Draw students' attention to the Lerntipp and ask them to bring anything they find to the next lesson.

**Keys for Unit 8 – Part A**

**1.2** 1 more | 2 most | 3 less | 4 most difficult | 5 biggest | 6 unhappier

**2** 2 worse, the worst | 3 more boring, the most boring | 4 more anti-social, the most anti-social | 5 better, the best | 6 busier, the busiest | 7 more exciting, the most exciting

**3** (suggested answers) 1 better / less friendly | 2 more anti-social / busier | 3 best / worst | 4 more intelligent / worse at computing / better drivers | 5 best / worst ...

**4.1** 1 Audio, video and computers | 2 Flowers and plants

**5** 1 more | 2 most | 3 least | 4 less | 5 less | 6 more

**7.2 Nancy:** Masterchef, So You Think You Can Dance and Hell's Kitchen | **Joe:** nothing

**8.1** 1 E | 2 A | 3 C | 4 B | 5 F | 6 D

**9.1** Big Brother | The X Factor | The Apprentice

| Topics/Vocabulary | Life in the USA; an internet forum; travel tips for the USA; tipping |
|---|---|
| Grammar | Short answers; question tags |
| Functions | Agreeing and disagreeing; comparing dos and don'ts |
| Home study | Poetry in Motion; *I finally managed to speak to her* by Hal Sirowitz |
| Photocopiable | Page 65 |
| Extra materials | Class opener: A large map of the US; **3 Let's Talk:** A few pairs of scissors |

**Class opener** Ask students if they have ever been to the US and if so, where. Ask students to write the names of the places they've visited on the board. If nobody has been there, write down the names of five places in the US and ask the class if they know where they are located. You might want to show a large map of the US. Divide the class into two teams. Each team should think of three questions they can ask the other team which are associated with the places or sights or with anything else they know about the US. Encourage discussion to put together the questions and remind students of the information and dates they learned in Part A.

**1** **FOCUS** (V) *attitude, movements, environment, fuel efficient, argument* (P) *political, SUVs, efficient, neither*

**2 16** Move on to the questions in **(1)** and discuss as a class. For **(2)**, give students time to read through the statements before playing the recording. After checking the answers, go through the **Language Box** with the students and then ask them to turn to the audio transcript on p. 106 in the coursebook and to underline the different examples of agreeing/disagreeing.

Point out that *too* is only used when agreeing to a positive statement, whereas *neither* or *either* agree to a negative statement. To practise in class, ask students to provide simple statements of what they like and dislike which can be agreed/disagreed with and write them on the board. As a class, elicit possible short answers. Alternatively, go around the room or let a student make a statement and toss a ball to a classmate who must answer.

Some native speakers pronounce *neither* and *either* with a long *e*, whereas others pronounce them with a long *i*.

**2** **PRACTICE** (V) *priority, same-sex marriages, can't stand, career* (P) *career*

Students carry out **(1)** individually as presented in the coursebook and check their answers with a partner by reading the statements and responses. Students work in pairs for **(2)**. Be aware of the controversial topics that may result in strong opinions and use your judgment about opening a class discussion on one or two of the statements.

**3** **LET'S TALK** Ensure students find new partners before starting **(1)**. The pairs respond to these statements and when finished write down three statements of their own and cut them out and swap them with another pair, who leaves them face down on the table. One student picks a strip of paper and reads the statement to his or her partner, who then agrees or disagrees. Encourage further discussion on the statements. The statements are then swapped again with another pair. Students could find new partners again before doing **(2)** as presented in the coursebook.

**Optional photocopiable** Hand out a copy of the photocopiable to each student and ask them to fill in a short answer in agreement/disagreement with the statements. If students have had difficulty with the responses up to now, you could first have them mark all of the answers of agreement in the speech bubbles with one colour, and the answers of disagreement with another colour. Students could then take turns reading the statements to a partner, who then gives his or her answers. This could also be carried out in small groups.

**4** **FOCUS** (V) *to drop, in favor of, dumb/dumber, limit, to go low* (P) *dumb/dumber*

Carry out **(1)** as presented in the coursebook. Have students use a clean, full-sized piece of paper for **(2)**. When they have finished writing out their responses for **(2)**, students then pass their piece of paper to the person on their left, who in turn writes his or her reaction to the comment. Have students pass around the pieces of paper, each time adding a comment, two or three more times before returning then to the person who wrote the initial comment.

Students often confuse the English word *programme* with the German. Remind them that this is *Sendung* and that *Programm* is *channel*.

**5** **PRACTICE** **(V)** *to react to*

Explain to students what question tags are by reading the examples in the **Language Box** and pointing out that it is the equivalent to the German *oder?* or other similar sentence endings. Especially for a weaker class, after reading through the Language Box you could ask students to find examples in 4 Focus. Proceed with **(1)** and **(2)** as presented in the coursebook.

 Collect more examples of question tags on the board by writing short sentences and then asking the students as a class to give the tag, e.g. *It can't be true, can it? / It doesn't rain here in the summer, does it?*

**6** **SOUND CHECK**
2 17
2 18

Do **(1)** as described in the coursebook. Allow students to read through the statements in **(2)**, then play the recording and have them tick the correct boxes. Check as a class. You could have students practise the intonation with a partner by reading out the statements in **(2)** or alternatively by reading the example sentences on the board from the Teaching Tip following 5 Practice.

**7** **OUT AND ABOUT** **(V)** *strangers, porter, to be understanding, to be seated*

Proceed with **(1)** as presented in the coursebook. Ask students if they were surprised by any of the results. At this point you could ask students for additional tips based on their experiences in the US. After having the students carry out **(2)** in small groups, compare as a class and make a table on the board.

**Homework suggestion** As optional homework, students could expand on the ideas in 7 Out and about to create a guidebook for their country and bring it to the next lesson. If you have a guidebook for their country, you could bring it to the next class or write down some things you find surprising and discuss these ideas with your students at the beginning of the next class. Point out the different sections for such a guidebook, e.g. *in a supermarket, in a restaurant, in the town.*

**8** **OUT AND ABOUT** **(V)** *to be supposed to, he couldn't help that* **(P)** *certainly*
2 19

Before playing the audio, ask students if they have ever eaten in a restaurant in the US or if they can name any restaurant chains or what sorts of restaurants they would expect to find there. If some students have dined in the US, ask them what they found to be different from restaurants in Germany. After giving students time to read through the dialogue, play the audio. Check answers in pairs, having students pay attention to correct intonation, and then refer them to the **Culture Tip**. Ask the students if they were aware of the facts mentioned and what they think of them.

**HOME STUDY**

Remind students to read the text and answer the questions. In the next lesson you could ask if anyone has brought a poem to share with the class.

---

**Keys for Unit 8 – Part B**

**1.2** 1 F I 2 F I 3 T

**2.1** 1 C I 2 A I 3 E I 4 B I 5 F I 6 D

**Language Box** You have a negative question tag after a positive sentence. I You have a positive question tag after a negative sentence.

**5.1** 1 Good health is more important than anything, isn't it? I 2 You can't buy friends or love with money, can you? I 3 You can buy a better education with money, can't you? I 4 The happiest people in the world have got lots of money, haven't they?

**6.2** 1 falling I 2 rising I 3 falling I 4 falling I 5 rising I 6 falling

**7.1** 1 false I 2 true I 3 false I 4 false I 5 true I 6 false

**8** 1 don't they I 2 doesn't it I 3 was it I 4 could he I 5 didn't he I 6 did it I 7 can he I 8 don't you

UNIT 9

# GETTING AROUND

## Part A Directions

| | |
|---|---|
| **Topics/Vocabulary** | Directions; theme parks |
| **Grammar** | Giving directions; conditional sentences (type 1) |
| **Functions** | Giving directions; checking to make sure you understand; talking about possibilities |
| **Home study** | Following directions; conditional sentences (type 1); prepositions |
| **Photocopiable** | Page 66 |
| **Extra materials** | **1 Focus, 2 Practice:** a transparency of the map on p. 74; **5 Let's Talk:** adhesive labels or nametags; **Photocopiable:** dice and figures |

**Class opener** Invite students to read out their poems from the Home study in Unit 8 Part B as well as their sentences explaining their selection. Review any questions that resulted from the Progress Check.

Write the words *theme park* on the board. Ask students to come up with adjectives that could be used to describe a theme park, e.g. *expensive, scary, fun*. Collect the words on the board. See if students can use the adjectives to describe an experience they've had at a theme park. Elicit which park it was and when they visited it.

**1 FOCUS** 2 21

(V) ***seal, walrus, honestly, lost and found, roller coaster*** (P) ***honestly, opposite***
Give students time to take a close look at the map in **(1)**. Have students discuss the question in **(1)** with a partner before sharing ideas with the class. You could ask each pair to pick one attraction to describe. Then go through the **Language Box** as a class. Before playing the recording, you could use an overhead transparency to project the map onto the wall or board. Carry out **(2)** as described, then invite a volunteer to trace the route on the projected map.

> ! German students may make several errors that deal with the concepts in 1 Focus, e.g. with *opposite* and *near*. Write the two words on the board and put a small cross at either side of each word to show that these are single words: you cannot say *opposite ~~from~~* or *~~in the~~ near ~~of~~*. A similar issue arises with *near* and *nearby*. Tell students that *nearby* is only used at the end of a sentence, e.g. *The Video Arcade is nearby*. Not *The Video Arcade is near~~by~~ the Information Center*. It might also be helpful to mention that *to take a photo* is correct, not *to ~~make~~ a photo*.

**2 PRACTICE**

Divide the class into pairs, then proceed as explained in the coursebook. Students should take it in turns to describe their positions. To extend the activity and practise the language for giving directions, see if students can describe how to get from the position the first student has chosen to the one his or her partner has chosen. The pairs could then share one of their examples with the class and illustrate their movements on the overhead transparency if one was used for 1 Focus.

**3 PRACTICE**

(V) ***intersection, pavement***
Proceed as in the coursebook and have students work individually or with a new partner. Elicit answers as a class and find out which combinations were already known and which were more difficult. As an extension, you could ask students if they know any other words which are different in British/American English, e.g. *caretaker/janitor, chips/fries, crisps/chips, trousers/pants*.

**4 PRACTICE** 2 22

Carry out the activity as presented, then play the recording and check answers as a class.

**5 LET'S TALK**

Introduce the phrases in **(1)**. You could start with the student to your left and ask each student to read one phrase out loud. Ensure that students have new partners for **(2)**. Proceed as in the coursebook, stressing the importance of trying to check the information with a partner and to practise using as many phrases as possible.

> ! To provide students with some practical experience giving and checking directions for locations they know, first ask each person to take a sticky note from you that is marked either A or B and to stick it on their shirt. Ask students to stand up and mingle. When you clap your hands, the students with A should greet the nearest person with a B label and ask that person how to get from the building they are in now to a place in the town that is not too far away. Repeat with B being the ones to ask a person wearing an A label. Students should retain their labels for 8 Let's Talk.

Now turn to the **Culture Tips**. Students should read the tips individually. Ask if there are any questions, and then ask for a volunteer to come up to the board and illustrate and explain the first tip. Another student should do the same for the second tip. Ask students if and/or how the rules differ in Germany or where they are from.

 **Optional photocopiable** Divide the students into groups of three or four. Give each group a board, dice and figures for the game. Students place their figures next to the square with the arrow (top left corner). One student begins by throwing the dice and moving clockwise around the board according to what it says on the dice. With the help of the time details given in the middle of the board, students formulate a question (*Where were you ... + preposition given on square + time*): *Where were you at half past two?* The next person answers by choosing a place from the middle of the board and adding a correct preposition (*I was ... + preposition + place*): *I was at the supermarket.* After answering, he or she continues by throwing the dice and asking the next student a question. This procedure continues around the board until everyone has had one or more opportunities to ask and answer a question.

 In English you say *in the Canaries, in Majorca* (large areas surrounded by water) but *on Key Biscayne, on the Isle of Man* (small areas surrounded by water).

**6**  **FOCUS** (V) *to beat the crowds, a waste of money, rush-hour traffic*
**2 23** Give students a few minutes to read the instructions and options in **(1)**. Play the recording, then elicit the answers as a class. Refer to the **Language Box** and write the first sentence on the board. Using different colours, write *simple present* under the *if* part of the sentence and *will future* under the second part. Go through the Language Box as a class and answer the question.

**7** **PRACTICE** Students write in the verbs individually and then check their answers with a neighbour. Review the answers as a class. Point out that many of the questions invert the clause order. In a weaker class, reinforce the structures by having students write down three sentences of their own, also using the inverted clause order.

 Point out that commas are only used in conditional sentences in English when the *if*-clause is in the first position.

**8** **LET'S TALK** If you used the Teaching Tip in 5 Let's Talk, you could have students choose a partner who has or is wearing the opposite label, A or B. Then the pairs should proceed as presented in the coursebook. Tell the students they should aim to write at least three questions. When both are finished forming the questions, they can ask each other the questions alternately, each giving a complete conditional sentence as an answer. When all pairs are finished, ask one person from each pair to report back to the class.

**HOME STUDY** Remind students to complete the Home study and challenge them to make a list of prepositions connected to directions as described in the Lerntipp. The lists could be compared at the beginning of the next class.

 **Keys for Unit 9 – Part A**

**1.2** The family starts in the *Seal and Walrus Stadium*. They should then turn right and walk past the pizza place and *The Barracuda*. They should turn left at the *Jellyfish Aquarium* and walk straight to the *Information Center*. The lost and found is in the Information Center opposite *Cap'n Silverbeard's Gift Shop*.

**3** 1 F I 2 H I 3 E I 4 A I 5 D I 6 G I 7 B I 8 C

**4** 1 straight I 2 turn I 3 on I 4 go I 5 take I 6 on

**6** 1 If we go now, we won't have time for the roller coaster. I 2 If we don't stay longer, we'll miss the Killer Whale Show. I 3 If Robyn has lunch first, she'll be sick on the roller coaster. I 4 If we leave by three o'clock, we'll miss the rush-hour traffic.

**7** 1 won't be I 2 ask I 3 won't finish I 4 visit I 5 will it cost I 6 doesn't hurry up

| Topics/Vocabulary | Plans; Graceland; an Elvis impersonator from Speyer |
| --- | --- |
| **Grammar** | Future with *going to* and *will* |
| **Functions** | Expressing intentions/plans; expressing spontaneous decisions |
| **Home study** | Hurricanes |
| **Photocopiable** | Page 67 |
| **Extra materials** | **Class opener:** pictures cut out of a magazine or copies of a map; |
| | **7 Out and about:** A4 pieces of paper, tape (optional) |

**Class opener** Hand out pictures of a town, street corner or intersection from a magazine, or copies of a map. Have the students, in pairs, write down a description of the places in the picture(s) or directions for going from one point to another on the map.

**1**  **FOCUS**
**2 24**

Clarify what is meant by *long weekend*, then carry out **(1)** as a class. Alternatively, **(1)** could be carried out in pairs which then report back to the whole group. Before moving on to **(2)**, tell students they are going to learn about the form *be going to*. Write a sentence on the board using the form, e.g. *After my English lesson I am going to meet a friend.* Underline *am going to meet*, and then look at the **Language Box**. As a class, go over the information and answer the question. Then direct students' attention to **(2)** and ask students to read through the dialogue and fill in their answers. Then play the recording so students can check their answers. Have the students work in pairs and see if they can answer the questions in **(3)** without hearing the recording again. Then check answers as a class. Finally, refer to the post-it note and elicit some examples from the class.

> When dealing with personal accounts such as in 1 Focus (1), do not force students to talk about their private holidays if they do not want to. Ask for volunteers who would like to offer their contributions.

**2** **PRACTICE**

**(V)** *dry-cleaner's*
Students should look at the picture and then the ideas. Check as a class to ensure the meanings of the linking words are clear. Tell students that no specific order is required: they can put the sentences into any order they want.

Alternatively, you could write the linking phrases on the board while the students are reading the sentences. Ask one student to write the first sentence in its *be going to* form on the board after *first of all*. He or she should choose another person to come up and pick a sentence of his or her choice and write it next to *then*. Continue in this way until the activity is complete. Encourage the use of *and* to help the sentences flow.

**Optional photocopiable**
**(V)** *appointment*
Students practise the *be going to* form by exchanging information in order to schedule an appointment. Hand out either the top or the bottom half of the page to each student; students find a partner with the other half and then work in pairs to figure out the two possible time slots.

**3** **LET'S TALK**

Ask students to work with a partner and proceed as in the coursebook. They should use this activity as a speaking activity, making only brief notes. When finished, they team up with another pair and have a conversation about their respective future plans.

**4** **FOCUS**
**2 25**

Have students read the instructions and then carry out the activity individually. Play the audio so the students can check their answers. Then go through the **Language Box** together and complete the statement about what is used in German. To reinforce the concept presented, you could write the following four sentences on the board and solicit possible responses from the class. 1. *I can't do this alone.* 2. *I have missed the last train.* 3. *I need one more copy of this worksheet.* 4. *I haven't got time to phone him.* In a weaker class, provide an example response for the first sentence such as *I'll help you.* When each sentence has a response on the board, underline the *'ll* in each case in another colour and emphasize that *will* + infinitive must be used.

**5** **PRACTICE** Use this activity to reiterate the explanation in the Language Box. Students could work individually or in pairs and then share some answers with the class.

**6** **LET'S TALK** (V) *recommendation, to recommend* verb+*ing*
Before forming small groups, go through some examples with the whole class. If 5 Practice was done in pairs, encourage the students to work with different people. Students could write down a few ideas before beginning, but try to keep this activity an oral one and encourage as much discussion as possible. Point out that the gerund is always used after *to recommend*. The most interesting or unusual recommendations could be reported back to the class.

**7** **OUT AND ABOUT** (V) *ultimate, pilgrimage, check out, acre, trophy, memorabilia, to display, ranch* (P) *ultimate, acre*
Give students time to read the text in **(1)** alone. Ask students for any vocabulary that is new to them. You could list these words on the board and see if they can figure out their meanings from the context. Proceed with **(2)** as in the coursebook. You could ask students to draw a mind map with Elvis in the middle and categories such as *person, songs, films*. Have the pairs report their findings to the class, present their mind maps, or put their mind maps on the wall or board. Alternatively, the contributions could also be compiled into one mind map on the board.

**8** **OUT AND ABOUT** **2 26** (V) *to be hooked, to slip into (a role), to entertain, material, introvert, conventions, anniversary*
Give students time to read the questions. Play the recording twice if necessary, and have students answer the questions as a class or in pairs. If in pairs, check the answers with the class.

**HOME STUDY** Point out the text on hurricanes in the Home study. Consolidate what was covered in Unit 9 by asking students to do C Writing for homework; offer to collect it for correction at the next class.

**Keys for Unit 9 – Part B**

**1.2** **2** going to stay **3** going to do **4** going to visit **5** going to drive **6** going to rent

**1.3** **1** He's going to Miami to visit a friend. **2** No, he's going to stay in a hotel. **3** He's going to drive down to the Everglades and rent bikes there.

**Language Box** You use *be going to* + infinitive to talk about plans in the future.

**4** **1** I'll have **2** I'll ask **3** I'll ask **4** I'll do

**Language Box** In German we use the present tense in these situations.

**5** (suggested answers) **2** I'll go to bed now. **3** I'll answer it / get it. **4** I'll have a cup of coffee, please. **5** I'll be there in a minute. **6** I'll help you.

**8** **1** He first heard an Elvis song on the day Elvis died. His dad bought a cassette on that day. **2** He has been to Graceland six times. **3** He describes himself as someone who interprets Elvis in his own way. **4** Dirk has three white suits, a red suit, a black leather one, a gold one and also an army suit like the one Elvis wore in the army. The suits cost between € 600 and € 2000. **5** Dirk performs at weddings, private parties, company events, and also at public events like festivals. **6** He is a quiet, more introverted person who likes listening to other people, the complete opposite to how he is on stage.

| Topics/Vocabulary | Christmas in Australia |
|---|---|
| **Grammar** | Present perfect and simple past |
| **Functions** | Talking about a holiday |
| **Home study** | Present perfect and simple past; vocabulary work |
| **Photocopiable** | Page 68 |
| **Extra materials** | None |

**Class opener**  To open the class you could refer to the Home study from Unit 9 and ask students to read out their emails from C Writing. Then give students a few minutes to write down two Christmas traditions they know about from other countries. Ask students for their ideas and write them up on the board. Keep the discussion brief.

**1  FOCUS**
**2 28**

(V) *to ring (s.o.), to chill out, awesome, seafood* (P) *awesome*

Transition from the Class opener by incorporating the questions in **(1)** into your discussion. Then turn to the **Language Box** on p. 83 and ask one student to read the present perfect sentences and another to read the simple past sentences out loud. Fill in the gaps in the Language Box with the class and review the formation of the two tenses. If needed, you could review the basic rules for each tense on the board and refer to what they learned in Unit 5 Part B. Now ask students to look at the conversation in **(2)** on p. 82 and work in pairs to complete the conversation. Then play the recording as in **(3)**. When they are finished, ask each pair to give one answer and to explain why they chose that tense. (The final two suggestions could also be carried out in reverse order.)

> Before continuing, to check the formation of positive and negative statements in both tenses, you could ask the pairs to write down two simple past sentences (one positive, one negative) and two for the present perfect. They could then swap with another pair and explain why they used the particular tense.

**2  PRACTICE**

(V) *illegal*

Give students time to complete the questions, referring them to the Language Box if required. Check their question constructions as a class. Students will have the opportunity to answer these questions verbally in 3 Let's Talk and should just concentrate on the question forms for now.

**3  LET'S TALK**

Before they write down the additional questions, remind students that they should consider whether the questions refer to unfinished time (present perfect) or to finished time (simple past). Walk around and check that students are focussing on the question type. Before the pairs begin speaking, you might want to go over Questions 1 and 2 in 2 Practice as a full class in order to review short answers appropriate for each tense.

> Be on the lookout for students who try to use a direct translation from German (*Have you ...?*) when forming questions for the simple past.

**4  SOUND CHECK**
**2 29**

Explain to students that, as in German, prefixes can be added to a word to change its meaning, e.g. *IM-possible*. Proceed with **(1)** as presented in the coursebook and check the answers. Carry out **(2)** as in the coursebook. Conclude by explaining to the class that the stress is on the main part of the word in English as opposed to being on the prefix as it is in German. To round off the activity and to give students an opportunity to say the words with the prefixes, students could form two or three sentences using the words in **(1)** and read them out to the class.

**5  FOCUS**

(V) *melted, attached, competition*

Give students time to read the email on their own and follow the instructions in **(1)**. When everyone has finished, ask one student to read out the email. Decide on a sound for the simple past (e.g. a knock on the table) and a sound for the present perfect (e.g. snapping of fingers). When the student who is reading says a verb that uses one of the two tenses, the others should make the appropriate sounds.

Move on to the **Language Box**, asking another student to read out the examples. Then fill in the gaps as a class. Go back through the email with the students and ask them to find the signal words presented in the Language Box. Point out that *yet* normally goes at the end of a sentence and *just*, *already*, *ever* and *never* go after the verb *have*. For **(2)**, students could work with a partner and write the correct tense above each signal word. Alternatively, you could write the two tenses on the board in two columns and ask students to come up and write the signal words in **(2)** under each heading.

You could ask your students to tell you the meaning of the *'s* in *it's become* and *it's a bit* in the last three lines of the email.

**6** **LET'S TALK** For **(1)**, ask students to take a clean piece of paper and to write out questions for the points listed in **(1)** about three lines apart. You could have them write several follow-up questions now or have them do that spontaneously when speaking with their classmates. Encourage students to mingle with their classmates with the aim of getting a positive answer and additional information for each question presented. Remind them to take notes so they can report their findings to the class as described in **(2)**.

To help students form the initial questions in the present perfect as well as the follow-up questions in simple past (using WH-questions), you might want to go over several examples using the first statement in the list in 6 Let's Talk **(1)** with the class before students carry out the speaking activity.

**Optional photocopiable** Students work in groups. Each group is given the photocopiable as a set of cards cut up prior to the lesson. The cards should be placed face down on the table. The first student picks up the top card and reads the sentence aloud. The others in the group have to decide whether the sentence on the card is present perfect or simple past. The answer appears on the card in brackets. Whoever says the right answer first keeps the card and reads out the next. If a wrong answer is given, the card is placed at the bottom of the pile. After correct answers have been given for each card, the students arrange the cards into thematically corresponding pairs (as they appear on the uncut photocopiable), and then compare them to discuss their different meanings.

You might like to hand out a copy of the uncut photocopiable to students at the end of the lesson so they can use it as a reference.

**HOME STUDY** Point out that students can practise the two tenses further in the Home study.

To close the lesson, draw their attention to the Lerntipp and discuss which films students might have already seen in English and how well they understood the story. Encourage students to either borrow or purchase a film before the next lesson or before the end of the course. Children's films are often a good start. Share any suggestions you have.

**Keys for Unit 10 – Part A**

**1.2** 3 got up | 4 've had | 5 Have you been | 6 Have you ever had | 7 had | 8 's been | 9 snowed | 10 have already built | 11 built | 12 haven't you sent

**Language Box** present perfect | simple past

**2** 3 Have you ever had a really unusual holiday? | 4 Where did you go the last time you flew? | 5 Did you meet any interesting people on your last holiday? | 6 Have you ever done anything illegal on holiday?

**4.1 and 4.2** (the stress is underlined) 1 fair – unfair | 2 usual – unusual | 3 practical –

impractical | 4 legal – illegal | 5 official – unofficial | 6 relevant – irrelevant

**5.1** Underline: Has ... melted / 've already taken / 've taken / 's become / haven't been | Circle: was / asked / did / Did ... know / designed / had / won

**Language Box** present perfect | simple past

**5.2** simple past: a few days ago, last year, on my birthday | present perfect: already, so far, this year, yet

## Part B Eating out

| | |
|---|---|
| **Topics/Vocabulary** | Ethnic food; Australia Day; in a restaurant |
| **Grammar** | *since/for* with the present perfect |
| **Functions** | Relating past events and experiences; ordering a meal |
| **Home study** | Art of the Aboriginal people |
| **Photocopiable** | Page 69 |
| **Extra materials** | **Class opener:** Small notecards or pieces of paper |

**Class opener** Hand out a piece of paper to each student and ask them to write down the names of their favourite foods when they go out to eat. They should not include where they eat them. Collect the pieces of paper – you will use them in 1 Focus (1).

**1 FOCUS**
**2 30**

(V) *to immigrate, to run a ... shop*

Continue from the Class opener by asking the class the question in **(1)**. Give everyone a chance to speak. Students should listen carefully to what the others say. Randomly hand out the pieces of paper from the Class opener and ask students to guess which piece of paper belongs to which person based on the contributions made in the discussion. Then have them read the instructions and questions in **(2)**. After playing the recording you could check the answers with the class and ask students to identify the difference between *for* and *since* based on their answers. Point out that both *for* and *since* answer the question *how long*. Draw attention to the **Language Box** and have students fill in the gaps. Check together.

Remembering the difference between *since* and *for* is not easy for German speakers. To help them, you can write the two words on the board. Make the dot on the *i* of *since* big and tell them this is a ZeitPUNKT. Separate the *r* of *for* by drawing a line before it and add the letters *aum* to make *Raum* for a ZeitRAUM.

**2 PRACTICE**

(V) *a couple of weeks*

Students could work individually or in pairs for **(1)**. After checking their answers with another pair or with the class, students then work individually to form sentences as presented in **(2)**. Be sure to point out that they are not limited to the time points and time periods given in **(1)** and also that they will give their sentences to another student to check. Students then swap sentences and check their classmates' sentences. To round off the activity, each student shares a sentence or two about him- or herself with the class. If the class is big, you could collect the sentences or go around and check as the students are checking their classmates' work.

**3 LET'S TALK**

(V) *present address*

Divide the class into groups of about four people, depending on class size, and encourage them to ask each other questions, concentrating on using the present perfect both when asking and answering. In a weaker class, you could have the students write out the questions prior to doing the speaking. Report back to the class group by group, first stating the answer to each question, and then giving specific details about how long people have done things, e.g. *Thomas has lived at his present address for 35 years*.

Draw attention to the *How about you?* question modelled in 3 Let's Talk to direct the question to another group member and maintain the flow of conversation.

**4 PRACTICE**

Begin this activity by asking students to give you the main uses of simple present, simple past and present perfect, including their respective signal words. If the group is weaker, write these as notes under each tense on the board. Give students time to fill in the gaps alone or with a partner and then compare with a partner or another pair before eliciting the answers as a class.

**5 LET'S TALK**

(V) *to be in business, swimmers* (Profile Card D)

Form new groups of four. Ask each student to choose a role, turn to the respective page, read the role and complete the profile card on p. 87 of the coursebook. Give students time to consider which questions they need to ask their classmates in order to complete the other profile cards on p. 87. Encourage the students to spell out any names so the group members can correctly complete the cards. It's important to make sure the groups have enough time to exchange the profile information as well as to answer the questions above the profile cards. With the class, review the answers to the general questions, and then ask each group to report which restaurant they selected.

**6**  **(V)** *settlement, spicy, mustard* **(P)** *mustard, barramundi*

After giving the students time to read the instructions to **(1)**, have students read through the menu and find any words they are not sure of. Help with vocabulary as needed. Then students could work individually or with a partner to complete the gaps. Check answers as a class. For **(2)**, form groups of three. Mention that they might like to include drinks on their menus. It may be necessary to assist with the vocabulary for ingredients or dishes as the groups work. Make a note of the words they don't know. At the end of the activity, you could write the words on the board. Note that the menus the students created in **(2)** will be used in 7 Out and about **(2)**. The groups should be retained as well.

**7**  **(V)** *starter, main course*

For **(1)**, give students time to read the conversation and fill in the gaps. Play the recording and allow students to check their own answers. In **(2)**, the groups swap menus from 6 Out and about (2) and choose one person to be the waiter/waitress and proceed with the role-play. When each group has completed the role-play, one person from each group should report back to the class on what they thought of the menu they received and each person should name his or her choice of dish. Finally, refer to the **Culture Tip**, explaining that this type of restaurant is normal in many parts of Australia. You could also ask if the students have ever been to such a restaurant and what they think of the concept of BYO and a corkage fee.

> Point out the difference between *I would like ...*, and *I like ...* Explain that if you only say *I like*, you express that you think something is good, but not that you want it.

**Optional photocopiable**  Provide a copy of the photocopiable to each student. Students could work in groups, pairs or individually for **(1)** and **(2)** and could then compare answers before checking in the class. If the class works in groups or pairs, you could provide a prize to the group or pair that got the most answers correct.

**HOME STUDY**  Encourage students to look at the text about Aboriginals at home and do A Reading and B Vocabulary. If you see your students again after this lesson, remind them you will collect C Writing. Alternatively, do C Writing as a class to round off the course.

### Keys for Unit 10 – Part B

**1.2**  **1** For over 50 years. **2** Since 1999. **3** For two years.

**Language Box**  since **i** for

**2.1**  **for:** a couple of weeks, ages, as long as I can remember, five years, months, ten minutes **i since:** 2007, I left school, May, Monday, my birthday, nine o'clock, the party

**4**  **1** left **2** lived **3** lives, runs **4** has been, has had **5** worked **6** stopped **7** has been, has played **8** plays, does

**5**  Topolinos has been in business the longest. Topolinos has been at its present address the longest. The Thai Thani serves only traditional food.

**6.1**  **1** tomato **2** nuts and toast **3** grilled **4** spicy coconut milk sauce **5** dips and vegetables **6** brownies

**7.1**  **1** Are you ready to order? **2** I'd like the **3** as a starter **4** Would you like a starter? **5** I'll have a beer

a girlfriend?

an English dictionary?

from the Caribbean?

play an instrument?

married?

a non-smoker?

sing well?

drive?

two sisters?

a good swimmer?

much time for your hobbies?

ride a horse?

a house?

older than me?

a coffee drinker?

cook British food?

a good tennis player?

speak another language?

a new car?

British?

✂ - - - - - - - - - - - - - - - - - - - - - - - - - - - - - - - - - - - - - - - - - - - - - - - - - - - - - - - - - - - - - - - - -

| Have you got ...? | Are you ...? | Can you ...? |
| --- | --- | --- |
|  |  |  |
|  |  |  |
|  |  |  |
|  |  |  |
|  |  |  |
|  |  |  |
|  |  |  |
|  |  |  |

## Room 1

## Room 2

## Part A  What about you? Do you ...?

**Tick what is right for you:** yes no

love Indian food ☐ ☐

speak French fluently ☐ ☐

always drive carefully ☐ ☐

often go to football matches ☐ ☐

usually clean the kitchen ☐ ☐

like spiders ☐ ☐

watch soap operas ☐ ☐

hate doing the shopping ☐ ☐

✂------------------------------------------------------------------------

**Tick what is right for you:** yes no

love Indian food ☐ ☐

speak French fluently ☐ ☐

always drive carefully ☐ ☐

often go to football matches ☐ ☐

usually clean the kitchen ☐ ☐

like spiders ☐ ☐

watch soap operas ☐ ☐

hate doing the shopping ☐ ☐

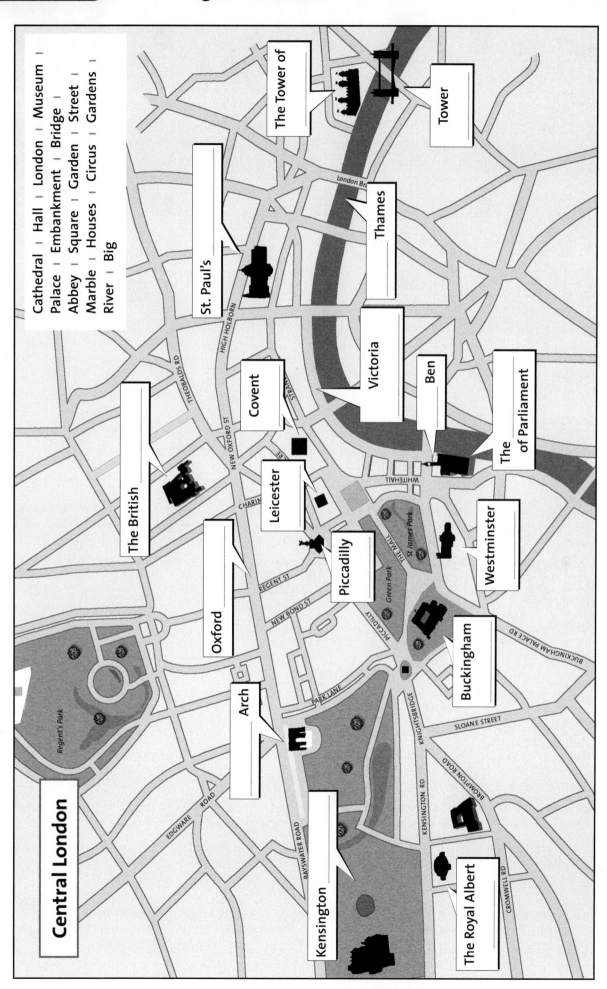

Cathedral ⎪ Hall ⎪ London ⎪ Museum ⎪
Palace ⎪ Embankment ⎪ Bridge ⎪
Abbey ⎪ Square ⎪ Garden ⎪ Street ⎪
Marble ⎪ Houses ⎪ Circus ⎪ Gardens ⎪
River ⎪ Big

**Central London**

The Tower of _____

_____ Tower

_____ Thames

St. Paul's _____

Victoria _____

_____ Ben

The _____ of Parliament

Covent _____

Leicester _____

Westminster _____

The British _____

Piccadilly _____

Oxford _____

Buckingham _____

Arch

Kensington _____

The Royal Albert _____

| | | | |
|---|---|---|---|
| A woman is doing aerobics. She's bending her knees. | A boy is walking along the road. He is carrying a schoolbag. | A bird is sitting in a cage. It is singing. | A woman is sitting in an armchair. She's reading the paper. |
| Two boys are playing football. They are running after the ball. | A little boy is skating on a pond. He is wearing a scarf and gloves. | A mouse is hiding in a corner. It is eating some cheese. | A dog is sitting in front of the kennel. It is barking. |
| A woman is cycling. She's wearing a crash helmet. | A man is sitting at his computer. He's yawning. | A woman is standing in a shop. She is talking to the shop assistant. | A cat is lying on a chair. It is sleeping. |
| An old man is sitting in front of the telly. He's watching TV. | Two men are wearing big hats and they are smoking. | A little girl is walking out of a shop. She is carrying a bottle of milk. | A man is sitting in a restaurant. He's having a glass of beer. |

**Part B  What do you think about … ?**

**Ask as many of your fellow students as possible and write down their names:**

| What do you think about … | love | like | hate |
|---|---|---|---|
| … getting up early? | | | |
| … vacuuming? | | | |
| … _____ ? | | | |
| … _____ ? | | | |

*Oh, I really love ironing, especially in front of the telly.*

*Well, I hate driving, but I love taking the train.*

✂ - - - - - - - - - - - - - - - - - - - - - - - - - - - - - - - - - - - - - - - - - - - - - - - - - - -

**Ask as many of your fellow students as possible and write down their names:**

| What do you think about … | love | like | hate |
|---|---|---|---|
| … watching DVDs? | | | |
| … cleaning the bathroom? | | | |
| … _____ ? | | | |
| … _____ ? | | | |

*I like walking the dog when the weather is nice.*

| | You | Your Partner | Scoring (if the answer is 'yes') |
|---|---|---|---|
| 1  Did you manage to get a cheap flight/cheap accommodation? | | | 2 |
| 2  Did you like your accommodation? | | | 4 |
| 3  Did you have a stress-free journey? | | | 3 |
| 4  Did you enjoy the food? | | | 3 |
| 5  Did you meet interesting people? | | | 2 |
| 6  Did you practise your English? | | | 2 |
| 7  Did you have nice weather? | | | 3 |
| 8  Did you visit any interesting museums or exhibitions? | | | 2 |
| 9  Did you go swimming or jogging? | | | 4 |
| 10  Did you learn anything new? | | | 4 |
| 11  Did you watch a lot of TV? | | | 1 |
| 12  Did you sleep in when you felt like it? | | | 2 |

**Scoring**

| 32–24: | You must have had the perfect holiday! |
|---|---|
| 24–16: | That sounds like a really good holiday. |
| 16–8: | Not bad! |
| 8 and less: | Oh dear, that doesn't sound like a dream holiday at all. What a shame! |

| | |
|---|---|
| Nice to meet you. | Nice to meet you, too. |
| Nice to see you. | Nice to see you, too. |
| It was nice to meet you. | It was nice to meet you, too. |
| How do you do? | How do you do? |
| How are you? | Fine, thank you. |
| How are you doing? | I'm doing fine, thanks. |
| Thank you. | You're welcome. / Not at all. / No problem. |
| I hope it wasn't too much trouble. | Not at all. / No trouble at all. |
| *sneeze* | Bless you. / Gesundheit. |
| What do you do? | I'm a bartender. |
| What did you do? | We went to a pub. |
| What are you doing? | I'm sitting in English class. |
| Sorry. | That's okay. / No problem. / No worries. |
| Have a nice weekend. | Thanks, you too. |
| I have the flu and can't come today. | Get well soon. / Hope you feel better soon! |
| Enjoy your meal. | Thank you, you too. |
| I've just won the pub quiz. | Congratulations! |
| I must work overtime at the weekend. | Oh, that's a shame. |

## Part A  In a department store

A good friend / Your (grand)son or (grand)daughter is moving into a new flat and has made a wish list of things they need/want. Look at the store floor plan and the wish list below, then discuss with a partner which things you can find in which departments and how much you expect them to cost. Then join another pair and answer the questions at the bottom of the page.

*"Where can we get...?"*

*"I think we can find ... in the ... department."*

*"I think we can find ... on the ... floor."*

*"... will cost ..."*

**GROUND FLOOR**
menswear ǀ
men's shoes & accessories ǀ
wine department & cigar
shop ǀ gift wrapping service

**1st FLOOR**
food hall ǀ
jewellery & watches ǀ
beauty & perfumes ǀ florist

**2nd FLOOR**
womenswear ǀ women's
shoes & accessories ǀ
glasses & sunglasses

**3rd FLOOR**
tableware ǀ home
decoration & accessories ǀ
kitchenware ǀ books, pens
and stationery ǀ
travel goods

**4th FLOOR**
furniture ǀ bed & bath ǀ toys
ǀ childrenswear ǀ
sportswear & swimwear ǀ
sports equipment

**5th FLOOR**
technology ǀ tools ǀ pets ǀ
gardening equipment

### WISH LIST

a set of cooking pots

an electric kettle

nice towels

a cosy armchair

some pillows

fridge magnets

a pair of slippers

a screwdriver and a hammer

a multifunction printer

a funny apron and oven gloves

a key ring

kitchen knives

loudspeakers for an MP3 player

a coat rack

playing cards

an alarm clock

a picture frame

a fluffy bathrobe

1  What else would you put on the list? What is the standard equipment a flat should have?
2  What would make a good housewarming* gift? What are traditional housewarming gifts in your area?
3  Which of the other departments would you like to visit?

*celebrating moving into a new home

### Part B  How long ...? / Since when ...?

## Partner A

| Mary | be married / for 25 years. | have a driving licence / since last week. | want / to pass her driving test since her teenage years. |
|---|---|---|---|
| Peter | How long / be unemployed? | How long / belong to his chess club? | Since when / know his best friend? |
| Simon | be sick / since his new boss arrived. | enjoy / learning French for a year. | own / his house for two months. |
| The Harveys | Since when / have a new car? | How long / wish to have a garage? | Since when / dislike their neighbours? |

✂ - - - - - - - - - - - - - - - - - - - - - - - - - - - - - - - - - - - - - - - - - - - - - - - - - - - - - - - - - - - - - - - - - - - -

## Partner B

| Mary | How long / be married? | Since when / have a driving licence? | Since when / want to pass her driving test? |
|---|---|---|---|
| Peter | be unemployed / for a long time. | belong / to his chess club for ages. | know / his best friend since childhood. |
| Simon | Since when / be sick? | How long / enjoy learning French? | How long / own his house? |
| The Harveys | have a new car / since yesterday. | wish / to have a garage for as long as they can remember. | dislike / their neighbours ever since they met them. |

**Describe the pictures. Make sentences with *used to ...* and *now*.**

She used to live in Paris when she was young. Now she lives in London.

---

**1**

**2**

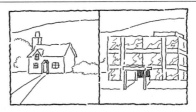

**3**

to be bald –
*eine Glatze haben*

**4**

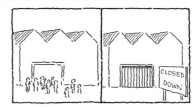

CLOSED DOWN

**5**

**6**

**7**

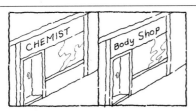

CHEMIST    Body Shop

**8**

| | |
|---|---|
| doing crosswords | checking the time |
| reading the newspaper | kicking the computer |
| cleaning my desk | doing a yoga exercise |
| throwing away old documents | closing the window |
| having a cup of coffee | smoking a cigarette |
| searching for something in my bag | chatting/gossiping with colleagues |
| counting my change | looking out the window |
| texting my friend | chewing on my pencil |
| dreaming of my holidays | dialling a number |
| talking on the phone | scratching my nose |
| staring at the monitor | sharpening my pencils |
| sleeping in my chair | eating a chocolate bar |

## Part A Reminders for travellers

have to I has to I should I don't have to I mustn't I shouldn't

1 You _____ pack your bag in time.

2 You _____ forget your passport and your ticket.

3 You _____ be at the airport two hours before the departure of your plane.

4 You _____ check in your luggage.

5 You _____ pay an extra charge if your luggage doesn't weigh more than 20 kg.

6 Your hand luggage _____ be scanned for security reasons.

7 You _____ carry any sharp objects on your person or in your hand luggage.

8 You _____ show your passport at passport control.

9 You _____ leave the departure lounge after going through passport control.

10 You _____ show your boarding card when you buy something at the duty-free shop.

11 You _____ put your luggage in the locker above your seat or under the seat in front of you.

12 You _____ stand in the aisle and block the way for the cabin crew and other passengers.

13 You _____ listen to the safety instructions given by the cabin crew.

14 You _____ smoke on board during the flight.

15 You _____ eat more than your stomach can take just because the food is free.

16 You _____ only leave your seat when it is really necessary.

17 You _____ use your mobile phone during the flight.

18 You _____ be polite and friendly to the cabin crew.

19 You _____ have a look at the duty-free catalogue before you buy something.

20 You _____ fasten your seatbelt before the plane takes off.

21 You _____ remain seated with your seatbelt fastened while the plane is landing.

22 You _____ have your seatbelt fastened all the time.

## Part B  Predicting the future

You will interview a partner about his or her predictions for the future.
First complete the mind maps with different topics. Then ask your partner for his or her predictions.

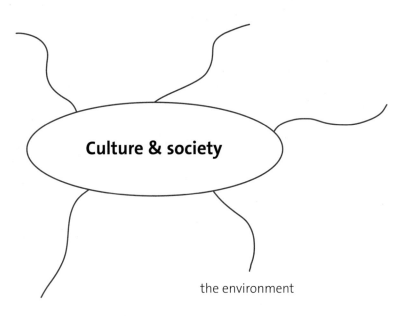

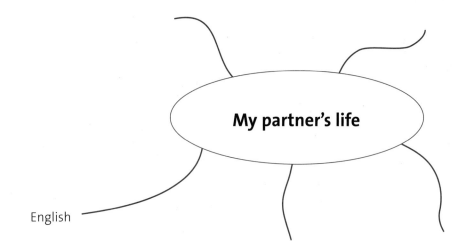

# PHOTOCOPIABLE 15

## Part A  Murphy's Law

**Everyone talks about Murphy's Law, but do you really know what it is? Murphy's Law is a general statement which tells us that 'anything that can go wrong, will go wrong'.**

Below are some interesting examples of what that can mean in everyday life. Match the sentence halves to find out what they are.

1  If there is a possibility of several things going wrong,  ☐

2  Everything takes longer  ☐

3  If you're looking for more than one thing,  ☐

4  Your best golf shots always occur  ☐

5  Those who know the least  ☐

6  Chaos always wins,  ☐

7  Behind every little problem there's a larger problem,  ☐

8  The file you are looking for  ☐

9  The person ahead of you in the queue  ☐

10  Your car keys are always in the pocket of the hand  ☐

11  If you're stuck in a traffic jam and you move to the fast lane,  ☐

12  The best things in life are free –  ☐

A  it will become the slowest lane; if you move back, that lane will stand still.
B  the one that will cause the most damage will be the one to go wrong.
C  will always know it the loudest.
D  when playing alone.
E  is always at the bottom of the largest pile.
F  than you think.
G  that is fullest.
H  you'll find the most important one last.
I  and worth every penny of it.
J  will have the most complex transaction possible.
K  because it's better organized.
L  waiting for the little problem to get out of the way.

**What about you?**
**Can you think of an everyday Murphy's Law situation yourself?**

## Part B  Short answers: agreeing

Read the statements 1–15 and express your agreement using short answers only. If you need help, look at the suggestions in the speech bubbles below.

Examples

*I believe the world is flat.*          *So do I. / I agree. / Good point.*
*I don't agree with low taxes.*          *Neither do I. / I don't either.*

1  I believe that I should have more rights than anybody else.          _____

2  I think we should always eat bananas with cheese on Tuesdays.          _____

3  I think our website is the most wonderful in the world.          _____

4  I'm against free weekends.          _____

5  Our Treasury Secretary (AE for 'finance minister') should be sent to prison.          _____

6  Seeing friends is a waste of time.          _____

7  I won't vote for the purple party.          _____

8  I believe that freedom of speech is important in politics.          _____

9  Our new party should spend all donations on lottery tickets.          _____

10  We will win next year's election.          _____

11  I can't stand coffee in the morning.          _____

12  I don't think our political rivals will win.          _____

13  I wouldn't support holiday trips to the moon.          _____

14  I am not in favour of supporting the Arts.          _____

15  I can't understand why we didn't get enough votes!          _____

So do I.          (Yes,) I agree.          Neither will I.          Yes, he/she should.          So we will.

I believe that/so too.          I think so too.          Neither can I.          Neither am I.          Neither would I.

Yes, we should.          Right.          I can't either.          Good point.          I don't either.

I'm not either.          I won't either.

Yes, it is.          So am I.          I wouldn't either.          Neither do I.

## Part A Where were you ...? (Prepositions)

**Start**

on the board:

in · on · at · no preposition · in · on · at

no preposition · in · no preposition · at · on · in · no preposition · at · on · in · no preposition · at · on · in

no preposition · at · on · in · no preposition · at · on · in

**Time**
May (or any other month) 2003
(or any other year) I Christmas Day I
Easter I half past two I last Thursday
(or any other day) I this morning I
September 18th (or any other date) I
the summer (or any other season) I
the weekend I three days / a week ago I
a few hours ago I Wednesday evening
(or any other evening) I lunchtime I
your birthday

**Place**
Britain/Italy (or any other country) I
home I bed I Majorca / the Canaries /
Key Biscayne (or any other island) I
Florida (or any other state) I
Edinburgh (or any other city) I
the motorway I the doctor's I the airport I
work I the bus stop I the office I
the supermarket I the post office I
a/the plane I a hotel I a business trip I
the station I a restaurant I the beach I
my desk I the bus I the (North Sea) coast I
a fun park I the shower I my/the living
room I my way to work I abroad

## Part B  Scheduling an appointment

### Student A

|  | Monday | Tuesday | Wednesday | Thursday | Friday |
|---|---|---|---|---|---|
| **Morning** | | Attend yoga class | | | Hike in the forest |
| **Afternoon** | | Have coffee and cake with a friend | Have lunch with a friend | Go food shopping at the outdoor market | |
| **Evening** | Look after the children/ grandchildren | | | Go to the cinema | Attend a friend's birthday party |

*What about Monday morning? We could meet then.*

*Sorry, I'm helping at the library. How about Wednesday afternoon?*

✂ - - - - - - - - - - - - - - - - - - - - - - - - - - - - - - - - - - - - - - - - - - - - - - - - - - - - - - - - - - - - - - - - - - - - - - - - - - - - - - - - - - - -

### Student B

|  | Monday | Tuesday | Wednesday | Thursday | Friday |
|---|---|---|---|---|---|
| **Morning** | Attend Zumba class | | Go swimming | | |
| **Afternoon** | Have lunch with a friend | Have coffee and cake with a friend | | Have coffee and cake with a friend | Look after the children/ grandchildren |
| **Evening** | | | Attend the theatre | Have dinner in the city | |

*What about Monday morning? We could meet then.*

*Sorry, I'm helping at the library. How about Wednesday afternoon?*

## Part A  Present perfect or simple past?

| | |
|---|---|
| How long have you lived here? *(present perfect)* | How long did you live there? *(simple past)* |
| I've never been to Sydney. *(present perfect)* | Last week we went to Sydney. *(simple past)* |
| I've known them for ages. *(present perfect)* | I first met him a year ago. *(simple past)* |
| We've been there once or twice. *(present perfect)* | We were there yesterday. *(simple past)* |
| I haven't seen him for a long time. *(present perfect)* | I saw him in town some days ago. *(simple past)* |
| He hasn't been in his office this week. *(present perfect)* | He wasn't in his office last week. *(simple past)* |
| I've learned English for some months. *(present perfect)* | I learned English at school. *(simple past)* |
| I haven't read his new novel yet. *(present perfect)* | I read his new novel on the train. *(simple past)* |
| Have you ever had Australian food? *(present perfect)* | Did you try Australian food when you were there? *(simple past)* |
| Have you learnt any new Australian words yet? *(present perfect)* | When I was on holiday in Australia, I had problems understanding some people. *(simple past)* |
| I haven't had any problems so far. *(present perfect)* | We didn't have any problems at the airport. *(simple past)* |
| Have you ever thrown a boomerang? *(present perfect)* | I threw a boomerang yesterday but it didn't come back. *(simple past)* |
| Have you ever stroked a kangaroo? *(present perfect)* | We stroked a kangaroo in the zoo in Sydney. *(simple past)* |

**1  Guess which of these sentences are true and which are false. Underline the comparative and the superlative forms. Then use these forms to correct the false statements.**

|  | | true | false |
|---|---|---|---|
| 1 | The summers in New Zealand are more pleasant than those in Australia. | ☐ | ☐ |
| 2 | New Zealand consists of the North Island and the South Island and the biggest volcanoes are on the South Island. | ☐ | ☐ |
| 3 | More people live on the South Island than on the North Island. | ☐ | ☐ |
| 4 | Wellington has been the capital of New Zealand since 1865 and it is one of the busiest ports there. | ☐ | ☐ |
| 5 | There are fewer spiders in Australia than in Germany. | ☐ | ☐ |
| 6 | As New Zealand belongs to the southern hemisphere, the north is warmer than the south. | ☐ | ☐ |
| 7 | January is the coldest and July the warmest month in New Zealand. | ☐ | ☐ |
| 8 | The kiwi is one of the most unusual birds and is only found in New Zealand. | ☐ | ☐ |
| 9 | Cricket is better known in the United States than in Australia. | ☐ | ☐ |
| 10 | The Maoris are one of the largest ethnic groups in Australia. | ☐ | ☐ |

**2  Tick the correct answer.**

1  What do the white stars on the right hand side of the Australian flag represent?
   A  eucalyptus flowers ☐
   B  the Southern Cross ('das Kreuz des Südens') ☐
   C  the number of states in Australia ☐

2  The writer Katherine Mansfield and the singer Kiri te Kanawa were both born in ...
   A  Tasmania ☐
   B  Australia ☐
   C  New Zealand ☐

3  What is the Australian currency?
   A  US dollars ☐
   B  Australian pounds ☐
   C  Australian dollars ☐

4  When is Australia Day?
   A  26th January ☐
   B  3rd March ☐
   C  4th July ☐

5  What was the nationality of the man who designed the Sydney Opera House?
   A  Danish ☐
   B  British ☐
   C  Australian ☐

6  What famous musical instrument do the Aborigines play?
   A  the bagpipes ☐
   B  the pan pipes ☐
   C  the didgeridoo ☐

7  Which animal can't you find in Australia?
   A  koala ☐
   B  crocodile ☐
   C  brown bear ☐

8  What is the population of Australia?
   A  30.1 million ☐
   B  20.4 million ☐
   C  25.2 million ☐

9  What is the capital of Australia?
   A  Sydney ☐
   B  Canberra ☐
   C  Melbourne ☐

10  What is the capital of New Zealand?
   A  Wellington ☐
   B  Christchurch ☐
   C  Auckland ☐

## PHOTOCOPIABLE 1
### Unit 1, Part A

**Have you got:** a girlfriend; an English dictionary; two sisters; much time for your hobbies; a house; a new car?

**Are you:** from the Caribbean; married; a non-smoker; a good swimmer; older than me; a coffee drinker; a good tennis player; British?

**Can you:** play an instrument; drive; sing well; ride a horse; cook British food; speak another language?

## PHOTOCOPIABLE 2
### Unit 1, Part B

In Room 2, there isn't a chair, a newspaper, a clock, a rug, a picture on the wall; there is only one coffee cup and there is only one plant.

## PHOTOCOPIABLE 4
### Unit 2, Part B

St Paul's Cathedral
The Royal Albert Hall
The Tower of London
The British Museum
Buckingham Palace
Victoria Embankment
Tower Bridge
Westminster Abbey
Leicester Square

Covent Garden
Oxford Street
Marble Arch
The Houses of
Parliament
Piccadilly Circus
Kensington Gardens
River Thames
Big Ben

## PHOTOCOPIABLE 5
### Unit 3, Part A

1 A woman is doing aerobics. She's bending her knees.
2 Two boys are playing football. They are running after the ball.
3 A woman is cycling. She's wearing a crash helmet
4 An old man is sitting in front of the telly. He's watching TV.
5 A boy is walking along the road. He is carrying a schoolbag.
6 A little boy is skating on a pond. He is wearing a scarf and gloves.
7 A man is sitting at his computer. He's yawning.
8 Two men are wearing big hats and they are smoking.
9 A bird is sitting in a cage. It is singing.
10 A mouse is hiding in a corner. It is eating some cheese.
11 A woman is standing in a shop. She is talking to the shop assistant.
12 A little girl is walking out of a shop. She is carrying a bottle of milk.
13 A woman is sitting in an armchair. She's reading the paper.
14 A dog is sitting in front of the kennel. It is barking.
15 A cat is lying on a chair. It is sleeping.
16 A man is sitting in a restaurant. He's having a glass of beer.

## PHOTOCOPIABLE 9
### Unit 5, Part A

a set of cooking pots – kitchenware
an electric kettle – kitchenware
nice towels – bed & bath
a cosy armchair – furniture
some pillows – home decoration & accessories
fridge magnets – kitchenware
a pair of slippers – bed & bath
a screwdriver and a hammer – tools
a multifunction printer – technology
a funny apron and oven gloves – kitchenware
a key ring – travel goods
kitchen knives – kitchenware/tableware
loudspeakers for an MP3 player – technology
a coat rack – home decoration & accessories / tools
playing cards – toys
an alarm clock – home decoration & accessories
a picture frame – home decoration & accessories
a fluffy bathrobe – bed & bath

## PHOTOCOPIABLE 10
### Unit 5, Part B

**Mary** How long as Mary been married? –
She has been married for 25 years.
Since when has she had a driving licence? –
She has had a driving licence since last week.
Since when has she wanted to pass her driving test? –
She has wanted to pass her driving test since her teenage years.

**Peter** How long has he been unemployed? –
He has been unemployed for a long time.
How long has he belonged to his chess club? –
He has belonged to his chess club for ages.
Since when has he known his best friend? –
He has known his best friend since childhood.

**Simon** Since when has he been sick? –
He has been sick since he new boss arrived.
How long has he enjoyed learning French? –
He has enjoyed learning French for a year.
How long has he owned his house? –
He has owned his house for two months.

**The Harveys** Since when have the Harveys had a new car? –
They have had a new car since yesterday.
How long have they wished to have a garage? –
They have wished to have a garage for as long as they can remember.
Since when have they disliked their neighbours? –
They have disliked their neighbours ever since they met them.

## PHOTOCOPIABLE 11
### Unit 6, Part A

1  He used to play football when he was young. Now he plays golf.
2  There used to be an old house / an old school / a cottage. Now there is a modern building.
3  He used to have black hair. Now he is bald.
4  There used to be a supermarket / factory. Now it's closed down.
5  She used to smoke. Now she doesn't.
6  There used to be a parking lot. Now there is a playground.
7  There used to be a chemist. Now there is a body shop.
8  He used to have a car / go by car. Now he's got a bike / he goes by bike.

## PHOTOCOPIABLE 13
### Unit 7, Part A

1 should | 2 mustn't | 3 have to | 4 have to | 5 don't have to | 6 has to | 7 mustn't | 8 have to | 9 mustn't | 10 have to | 11 have to | 12 shouldn't | 13 should | 14 mustn't | 15 shouldn't | 16 should | 17 mustn't | 18 should | 19 should | 20 have to | 21 have to | 22 don't have to

## PHOTOCOPIABLE 15
### Unit 8, Part A

1 B | 2 F | 3 H | 4 D | 5 C | 6 K | 7 L | 8 E | 9 J | 10 G | 11 A | 12 I

## PHOTOCOPIABLE 16
### Unit 8, Part B

1  So do I. / I believe that/so too.
2  So do I. / Yes, I agree.
3  So do I. / I think so too.
4  So am I. / I agree.
5  Yes, he/she should. / I agree. / Right.
6  Yes, it is. / I think so too. / Good point.
7  Neither will I. / I won't either.
8  So do I. / I believe that/so too. / Good point.
9  Yes, we should. / I agree.
10  So we will. / Right.
11  Neither can I. / I can't either.
12  Neither do I. / I don't either.
13  Neither would I. / I wouldn't either.
14  Neither am I. / I'm not either.
15  Neither can I. / I can't either.

## PHOTOCOPIABLE 18
### Unit 9, Part B

The possibilities for an appointment are Tuesday evening and Thursday morning.

## PHOTOCOPIABLE 20
### Unit 10, Part B

### KEY 1

1  True – more pleasant
2  False. It consists of the North Island and the South Island and the biggest volcanoes are on the North Island.
3  False. More people live on the North Island than on the South Island. / Fewer people live on the South Island than on the North Island.
4  True – busiest
5  False. There are fewer spiders in Germany than in Australia. / There are more spiders in Australia than in Germany.
6  True – warmer
7  False. July is the coldest month and January is the warmest. / January is the warmest month and July is the coldest.
8  True – most unusual
9  False. Cricket is better known in Australia than in the United States.
10  False. The Maoris are one of the largest ethnic groups in New Zealand.

### KEY 2
1 B | 2 C | 3 C | 4 A | 5 A | 6 C | 7 C | 8 B | 9 B | 10 A